Connecting With Young Children:

Educating the Will

by
Stephen Spitalny

Connecting With YoungChildren: Educating the Will
Revised 2nd Edition

Published by Chamakanda Press

Cover photos by Tara Patterson.

9 781105 320828
ISBN 978-1-105-32082-8
90000

Acknowledgments

I am incredibly grateful for Rudolf Steiner's contributions to so many wide-ranging topics, as well as his suggestions and guidance for self development.

I am grateful for the many wonderful books that have found their way to me, and to the many independent brick-and-mortar bookstores where many of those books have jumped off of shelves into my hands.

Thanks to the many people whose ideas I have read, heard and digested and made indistinguishable from my 'own' ideas.

Special thanks to Margret Meyerkort and Dennis Klocek who showed by their example how to think for oneself, and how to put Steiner's ideas and practices into practice.

Thanks to everyone who encouraged me towards writing this book. Thanks to those who read and freely offered suggestions on my content and text, and to those who commented on the first edition. Many of your suggestions have been incorporated into this edition.

Finally, thanks to my own children and grandchildren, and the many other children I have had in my care over the years who showed me the way.

Contents

Introduction

Just like you, I mean to do well.
Margret Meyerkort - *I would put in italics so it goes with quote — appear mm wrote intro*

More and more it becomes clear to me that it is all about the will! The challenges we face as early childhood educators and parents of young children are, by and large, the result of the diminishing will capacities of the young children. One of the causes is the proliferation of technological gadgets that are promoted as necessary for modern life, and specifically those marketed for children. Consumer culture has conspired to deliver to the young child exactly what is most detrimental for its development (foods and gadgets) while advertising wizards spin these very same products in such a way that parents line up in droves to make sure their child is not left out. The gadgets (including video games of all sizes, cell phones, computers, home dvd players and electronic screens) take children away from their life of will activity. The so-called 'food' given to so many children is lacking in nutritional value and life energy. Food is the substance the digestive system (the metabolic system) has to work with. This is the sphere of the will in the physical body. Another factor is the way most adults relate to young children, especially in the realm of verbal communication.

Adults offer explanations and instructions and questions, questions, and more questions to the young child. This prematurely awakens the child in his thinking, and diverts him away from the developmental relating through the will. We see children who don't imitate, who haven't become master of their own body, and who don't (or can't) seem to do much of anything.

The engaged will of the adult is an antidote for this situation. The adult's will must be active both in what they are doing and in their thinking. The adult, in utilizing her will in thinking, can create situations that wake up the child's will forces that have been put to sleep or damaged. Through engaging ourselves in will activities we become makers and creators. We must become *makers* for the sake of the children - making gardens, toys, dolls, food, and so on. The will forces of the adult must exaggerate themselves, must 'over-engage' as it were, as example for the children to begin to imitate – imitate the activities, and imitate the adult's engagement of will forces.

Adversarial forces are attacking the human being at its most tender and formative stages, preventing the positive unfolding of new gifts from the spiritual world of which the children are the bearers. Our responsibility, as soon as we become aware of the situation, is to stand up for the protection of childhood. The children are the hope and the future, and they are not receiving the support they need in their most formative years; their true needs are not being met.

In the lectures given to the first Waldorf school teachers prior to the opening of the school in 1919, (*Study of Man*) Rudolf Steiner spoke over and over about the education of the will. This is THE essential pedagogical activity, even more so today, and especially for the young child.

This is not a book about nutrition and food and the needs of young children, though a thorough understanding of nutrition is essential for teachers and parents of young children. This is not a book about the damaging effects of electronic media on the physical and social development of the young child; that topic is addressed elsewhere. This is a book about how to communicate with young children in ways that recognize and support their stages of development, and it is about the adult consciously choosing her actions and responses; learning how to speak and how to act and thereby awakening in the will. The subject here is the education of the will of the adult. Adult self-education is a pedagogical tool for strengthening and educating the developing will of the young child.

As a longtime Waldorf kindergarten teacher, mentor, child, parent, grandparent, and human being, I have had much opportunity to observe firsthand many modes and styles of adult speaking with young children. In my work with young children over several decades, I have become aware of the challenges facing modern adults in relating to young children. I have overheard verbal interactions with adults and children that leave me shaking my head in wonder, sometimes laughing and sometimes crying. Along with the sensory attack on young children of screen media, and the non-nutritive attack of the "food" industry, the realm of adult speaking is the greatest challenge in the lives of young children. More and more parents and teachers are at a loss about how to speak with their children, about how to help the children develop skills for resolving conflicts, and about how to bring their values across to the children.

In the sharing of my ideas and observations there is a risk of seeming as if my ideas are the one and only way to think about the subjects at hand. I may come across as sounding like I think that I know something. What you will read in these pages are not recipes, instead I offer my experiences and actions I have chosen as catalyst to wake up your thinking in the realm of speaking. If you are reading this book, you already are curious and have questions about relating to young children through verbal communication. I hope what you find herein helps you on your way. In advance, I offer my apologies and recognize my shortcomings in sharing ideas and my seeming righteousness in how I express them. I am constantly trying to overcome the human affliction of thinking that my thoughts and ideas are the correct and only thoughts possible.

I also offer apology if in any way my presentation herein leads to the arising of thoughts or feelings of guilt or shame in you, the reader. That is not my intention. I would be happy if this book helped to make anyone more conscious and so able to overcome patterns of habitual speaking and acting. My purpose in writing this is to offer ideas and suggestions you might not have thought yet, and you are, of course, free to take up these suggestions or not. After your own reflection on these ideas, and if they resonate with you, they can become your ideas as well. Guilt toward the past in some ways inhibits taking up new ideas and changing the very habits one wants to change. I want to inspire your moving forward in the best ways you have decided for yourself based on all you have learned!

This book is also about the adult waking up in her will in the activity of relating - in a more and more conscious way - and it is about understanding the will activity driving the young child. It is about becoming conscious in realms where awareness may not shine so brightly, and putting human attention onto thinking and feeling and perceiving as a basis for choosing how to respond.

This book is an offer of support for those who want to become more conscious in the realm of communicating with young children. The necessary context is the whole landscape of human relating and connecting, and what it is to be a human being. Therefore this book is not just about communicating; it is about many aspects of the vast realm of connecting and relating. I have attempted to offer tools for developing capacities in the adult through self education for true human connecting so we can become shining examples for the children who are the future of our human society.

My goal is for this book to be a resource for the development of the will in adults who can in turn support the development of young children on their path towards an active life of will based on choices consciously made. I hope this book can serve as an awakener of the will for the caregivers of young children as part of a path of becoming human.

What is being human? What is the fundamental nature of the human being?

A common language and basic definitions are needed as a foundation for this book. My thinking about human development and early childhood stages is based on the spiritual scientific understanding articulated by Dr. Rudolf Steiner. In this approach the essential core, the true individuality of the human being is spirit, which enters into earthly life clothed, as it were, in a physical body which is built out of material substance and based on hereditary factors. One's spiritual individuality receives a physical body with which to reveal its gifts and unfold its destiny on earth. For the purposes of this book the term *I* is used to denote the higher self of the human being. Rudolf Steiner referred to this spirit essence as *ego*, but it is not to be confused with *ego*ism and self-centeredness. The *I* is the essential, central, spiritual core of an individuality that lives in the spiritual world before birth. The *I* experiences the world through the intermediary activity of the soul which receives various sense impressions and processes them, from within the physical body.

The physical body has needs and instincts that reveal themselves, and sense experiences it wants to respond to. And the *I* has a destiny it is trying to unfold. The **soul** lives as a dynamic interaction between the physical world of body and its surroundings, and the *I* itself. The soul lives in the meeting place of the spiritual *I* and the physical world. The soul of a human being is the life of desires, the realm of what one is attracted to and what one is repelled by. The soul is experienced in patterns of behavior, and even patterned ways of thinking. The activities of the soul are perceiving, thinking, feeling and willing. No more and no less.

But we can only speak truly of the spirit if we describe how it finds expression in conditions of consciousness. We can only speak truly of the soul if we show how it lives between sympathy and antipathy, and of the body if we conceive of it in actual forms. (R. Steiner, *Study of Man*, p. 124)

One other element of human existence still needs mentioning - life. The physical body is the material substance that we name our body. Without some enervating force or energy, it would be simply a lifeless body, a corpse. But it does have life, and that enlivening life energy has various names from various traditions. In Chinese medicine that life energy is called Xi, or Chi. From India comes the term prana. Rudolf Steiner named the forces that give life to the physical as the **etheric body**. This body of etheric energy has both maintenance qualities and formative qualities, which are especially active in young children. The etheric body is the realm of the immune system, of the flowing of the fluids within the physical, and of movement in general. This four-fold nature of the human being is a basic assumption underlying this writing.

Two great mysteries of the human being are the questions of the will and the etheric. What are they really, and how do they function? In the young child, these forces are most prominently at work, so the mystery is compounded in the realms this book attempts to address. My hope is that in the course of this book, a glimmer of understanding about the human will and etheric activity will arise for the reader.

Often in this writing I refer to the young child in the first seven years. This is approximate, as are all other age-defined stages. When I have forgotten to name the stage, or grown weary of repeated use of the term 'young child,' I simply left it out. But please note, this entire book is focused on the young child so

and

when I use the terms 'child' or 'children,' I am referring to the years between birth age seven. Also note; there are various stages of development between birth and seven years old. I have tried to specify but it may seem confusing at times exactly what age I am referring to. My apologies!

I have tried to be consistent in my use of pronouns in the hope of eliminating confusion; I have tried to use the masculine pronouns for referring to the young child, and feminine when referring to the adult. I am one of a very few men in the field of early childhood education, and realize the vast majority of kindergarten teachers are women. So it seems sensible to refer to the kindergarten teacher or other adult herein as 'her.'

I am interested in what you think about what I have presented in this book and would enjoy hearing your comments.

Until you say
" few men in the field" shed
this appears to be
written by M. M

Trust in yourself.
There are many secrets you haven't yet discovered.
Margret Meyerkort

Chapter 1

Relating

When you try to pick out anything by itself,
you find it hitched to everything in the universe.
John Muir

The most fundamental human activity is that of relating and connecting. The human being relates herself to the world, to other human beings, to spiritual beings and to herself - to all aspects of experience. Giving attention to the activity of connecting reveals it in all aspects of human life and experience. It is within the potential of the human being to choose what one puts attention upon; to what or to whom are we relating? One of the few aspects of our life we have any control over is where our attention is focused.

To be social means to relate to the other. Relating is the realm of give and take; it is interactive. In our modern world human beings more and more experience isolation from each other, from the world of nature around them, and from the spiritual world. And most of all, human beings are disconnected from themselves. The human experience today is of fragmentation. In the ancient mystery centers and spiritual traditions the central practice was to *know thyself*. This is still the central task for a human being who chooses a path of self development.

For an parent or teacher or caregiver, the core principle is the meeting of the other, and to truly meet an other one must first know thyself. This is a core principle of Waldorf education.

The spiritual world where we live before birth is a social world where spiritual beings are connected and respond to each other. In the spiritual world, and even still at birth, one experiences a complete interconnectedness of everything. There is not yet an experience of self and other. As the child develops self-consciousness during his first years, and as his intellect gradually develops, there is more and more an experience of separation. The intellect is a gift, yet it also disconnects the human being from being fully 'present' and from the possibility of total engagement with objects or beings. Since the intellect is a reflective and objectifying capacity, it dis-engages us from all activity other than thinking. Many adults choose to embark on a spiritual path to be able once again to experience connection with the spirit and the spirit in the world around them and to overcome the separation created by the activity of the intellect.

A truly human education attempts to overcome this isolated quality of modern life by developing the capacities for connecting within each child, which will remain latent until later stages of life. We can plant the seeds in early childhood for faculties of relating but it is important to be conscious that we are working to nurture and fertilize what will bear fruits only in the child's later years. The task is to help the child relate to and connect with all aspects of life in ways suitable for their development, so that later as an adult many realms of connection are available to him. This is a social path toward cultural renewal and a more peaceful world, one individual at a time. If you want to change the world, change yourself so that when the children who imitate you grow up they will change the world.

You see if you really think out these matters in keeping with full reality, then you get a feeling of the immeasurable responsibilities connected with education and teaching. For you arrive at the following ideas: What I do with the child forms the adult beyond his twentieth year, and you see from this that one must understand the child, the complete course of life, not merely the age of childhood, if one wants to build up a real art of education. (Rudolf Steiner, *The Basel Course on Pedagogy*, April – May 1920, lecture 13, Also in *Understanding Young Children*, p. 52)

At birth, freshly coming from the spiritual world, one still experiences the complete interconnection of all and everything. There is not yet an experience of a difference between self and other for the young child. As the child develops self consciousness during its first years, and as its intellect gradually develops, there is more and more an experience of a separation, a development of an awareness of "This is me, and all the rest is not me." That is seen in various moments of the child's

development including, for instance when the personal pronoun
'I' is used to refer to itself, at the so-called nine-year change,
during adolescence and so on. It perhaps culminates at about
thirty five years of age with an experience of isolation and deep
longing for connection. Many adults choose to embark on a
spiritual path to be able once again to experience connection with
the spirit and the spirit in the world around them, and a true
connecting with other human beings.

*The most important thing is to establish an education through
which human beings learn once more how to live with one
another.* Rudolf Steiner, October 1922

The most important work with the young children is in the realm
of social life, the realm of relating. That is where much adult
energy must be devoted, and it can be exhausting. Yet is essential
for the future development of capacities in each individual child,
as well as a renewed social world. Developing habits in early
childhood of connecting with others opens the way for the
gradual discovery and recognition that there are other human
beings in the world who also have needs and desires and feelings.
The young child has a beginning awareness of self, yet it is a self
that is the center of the universe for them. As teachers and
parents, we can offer the children tools for a human way of
relating that can be taken up more and more consciously as they
get older. Essential in this is that we continually put before the
eye of our own consciousness the developmental stage of the
child. What sort of consciousness am I interacting with? Above
all we must welcome the child into the world with love and
attempt to see who it is that they are becoming.

*The first task to be achieved on the basis of anthroposophy in
education can therefore be that, to begin with, the aim is to see
that the teachers, the educators, are people who perceive the
human being in the deepest sense and, having developed this
attitude of genuinely observing the human being, approach the*

18

child with the love that results from such an attitude. (R. Steiner, *Human Values in Education*, p. 37)

As the experience of self develops in the individual and the intellect grows stronger, it pushes against the feeling of connection. The intellect functions by creating distance from what is being considered or observed, by objectifying what it is considering. As time has marched onward, systems of education have become more and more intellectual and thereby push children toward more and more disconnect, even in their thinking. It has pushed students away from ideals of true education. This has pushed education as institution away from truly educating.

The [truly] educated mind is the connected mind, connected to all manner of different human styles...connected to all sorts of complex experiences, some of them fraught with psychological and physical peril...; connected to a dizzying profusion of intellectual ideas which interconnect with one another, and in time, set the pulses racing with the sheer transcendence possible in the human prospect – a feeling like no other and sufficient to be its own reward without the candy prison of praise, gold stars, or the promise of future reward. Most of all,the educated mind is connected to itself. (John Taylor Gatto, *Weapons of Mass Instruction* p. 130)

What is *connection* but a two way relating in which one is open to what is coming from the other, and one is available to share with the other from their own inner nature. In relating we are interacting with the world and others and spirit, and it is based on our own sense of self. True connecting is a balanced interaction of giving and receiving, of speaking and listening, of offering and awaiting response, of sounding and silence. It is a true communicating, back and forth. It is empathy for the other, being able to stand in their shoes, as well as being able to transmit to the other what is your own experience, what is the content of your inner life. The deepest connecting is a dance between empathy and the revealing your inner self.

The further stage in cognition is attained by making the power of love a cognitive force. Only it must not be the shallow love of which alone, as a rule, our materialistic age speaks. It must be the love by which you can identify yourself with another being – a being to whom, in the physical world, you are not identical. You must really be able to feel what is passing in the other being just as you feel what is passing in yourself; you must be able to go out of yourself and live again in another... ... We can then experience the above identification with, and coming to life in, another being. Only then do we learn the highest degree of love which consists not in 'forgetting yourself' in a theoretical sense, but in being able to ignore oneself completely and enter into what is not oneself. (R. Steiner, *Anthroposophy, An Introduction* pps. 77-78)

Warmth is part and parcel of the activity of connecting. We are nurtured by the warmth of others, and we nurture others through our own warmth of openness, interest, attention, enthusiasm and true understanding. Then one can really see the other and give them the true feeling of being seen.

Chapter 2

The World of the Young Child and the Path of Becoming Human

The infant is totally dependent on his environment for everything. In other words, he completely entrusts himself to the environment with no reservations. When the warm sweet milk flows into his body he experiences satisfaction not only with the tongue and the back of the mouth; the whole body including the little kicking feet and tiny grasping hands, is involved in tasting. Tasting is done with the whole being; the soul opens out completely for the outside world with an all-pervading sense of delight. (Bernard Lievegoed, *Phases of Childhood*, p. 49)

A central developmental task for the young child is the growth of his own physical body. A new born baby has immature, "unfinished" internal organs - liver, heart, kidneys, brain, etc…, which must be properly formed. The form of the organs as well as their functioning need development. For example, breathing and pulse rates do not usually establish consistent rhythms until a child is six or seven years old. The eye muscles that focus while tracking take eight years to mature. At eleven or twelve years old the frontal lobes begin to be able to take charge of the cortex of the brain making logic and reasoning possible. To allow the child's forces of growth and formation to do their task without hindrance allows him to build a solid foundation for physical health throughout his life. These are the same forces that power the intellect, and as they are gradually released from their body forming activities, the intellect develops. However, the intellect can be forced into early functioning at the expense of the developing physical body.

What can be accomplished with forces available only at a later time should never be crammed into an earlier stage, unless one is prepared to damage the physical organism. (Rudolf Steiner, *Soul Economy and Waldorf Education)*

Looking at child development in terms of mental awareness or self-consciousness, there is a gradual awakening. The newborn can be described as asleep in terms of self-consciousness and awareness of the self and the world as separate. At this stage, the child and the world are a unity in the child's experience. All is one. All that is perceived by the child's senses are merely perceptions without connection to ideas or concepts. Concepts like 'mommy,' 'myself,' 'my hand,' have not arisen yet. The duality of self and other, of me and the world, only slowly appears. In the preschool and kindergarten years, the child lives in a sort of dream consciousness, not fully awake, as is an adult, to connecting his perceptions with concepts. This gradual awakening directly relates to the growth forces becoming released from their task of building up the body. These growth forces are the very same forces which are used for mental picture-making and memory, and for the functioning of the intellect.

What can be accomplished with forces available only at a later time should never be crammed into an earlier stage, unless one is prepared to damage the physical organism. (Rudolf Steiner, *Soul Economy and Waldorf Education)*

Pushing a child out of this dream consciousness prematurely into early intellectual awakening has adverse effects on his physical development that will manifest in the body later years. Allowing children to come to self-consciousness at their own pace is a gift for their future, a support for the development of their full potential.

Once upon a time there was someone who lived with many friends way up in the heavenly heights. The stars and planets were his friends as well. He had a favorite plaything. It was a ball of the purest gold. He liked to throw and catch it. Once he decided to see how far he could make it go so with all his might he set it soaring through the heavens. It sailed past the sun and moon and stars and planets until it landed in a big, white, puffy cloud. He went to the cloud and looked all over it, all around it, and he could not find his golden ball. So he reached into the cloud and he reached all around. He felt something smooth and round and hard. He pulled it out. It was his golden ball. But he noticed he had made a hole clear through the cloud. He peered down through the cloud and what he saw made him smile. He could see down to the earth below where children were laughing and singing, playing and dancing. He watched and watched and soon two tall people caught his attention. There was something about those two and he knew they had some things to teach him, and he had things to show them as well. So he turned to his angel and said. "I want to go down there to the earth, to be with those people."

His angel said, "You may go, but first you must visit your friends the stars and planets for they have special gifts for you." So he went to the sun, to the moon, to the other stars and planets, and they did indeed have gifts for him. When he had gathered all of his gifts, he returned to his angel who said, "I will keep your heaven clothes for you." And the angel sent his down, down, down to the earth below.

His Mommy caught him and carried him just below her heart for many months. His daddy had to wait alongside Mommy until the day he was born. When he was born, his mommy and daddy gave him a gift. It was his own name. And his name is Jack.
When Jack was born he could not run, he could not walk, and he could not stand or even sit up. When Jack was born he could not feed himself, and he could not speak the same language as mommy and daddy. There were so many things he had to learn in his first years. And today is Jack's fifth birthday. He is five years old. We'll have to wait and see what Jack will do now that he is five years old.

Imagine the spiritual world where a child lives before birth, picture a place of pure joy where the substance of each being is joy itself, each a drop of joy in the sea of joy. At some point, a longing arises, and a looking toward the earth, wanting to be there. A choice is made to incarnate, the spirit I decides to be born as a physical human being, bringing its gifts from the spiritual world. He is looking for a warm and loving welcome from his people. As a human being on earth there is much to be learned. Human life on earth is in fact the school for spiritual beings to develop toward their higher potential. In the choosing of parents, his spirit I sees there are things those particular adults have to offer him, and things it can bring to them from the spiritual world. He comes to a family where it is as if the instruction manual to each others' buttons is pre-programmed into the dynamic system. You can call that karma - a subconscious orientation to the 'buttons' or 'triggers' that set one another off. The incarnating being comes to earth and to human beings looking for warmth and welcoming and love, and to develop what he needs in his spirit I. When the infant is born, he is completely connected with everything and everyone in his environment. He is constantly amazed and in a state of continuous wonder towards all that he experiences.

Time and space are the only things that separate one thing from another. Take time and space out of the equation and what is left? Oneness! That's it! But even though one could say that time and space are illusions, they are important. They serve a purpose. Without them we would be unable to observe and experience individuality. The game would be over. (Victor Wooten, *The Music Lesson* p. 172)

Needs

The newborn has various needs that can only be met by other human beings since he is not yet able to care for himself. He has chosen to incarnate, to become a human being, with the expectation that these needs will be fulfilled by the adults to whom he is coming. These include the needs of the physical including the need to be fed, and the need to be cleaned and kept warm and dry. Additionally there are needs of the soul, the infant's soul, that can only be met by others. These include the need for attention, the need for affection and touch, and the need for acceptance and welcome. The infant also has a need for appreciation, of being met with the pure joy of the adult of being together with this new human being. The fulfillment of these needs is the basis for feelings of safety and security in the newborn. They are the basis for a trust in the world and in other people. And they are the practical basis for love.

Recent research shows how humans have a physiological need for touch that is related to mother/child bonding. There are also many positive effects of human-to-human touch that affect us throughout life. The skin is our largest organ, covering the whole body. If someone touches you, there is a pressure on the skin at the site of contact. Just under the skin are pressure receptors which send signals to the brain. The brain controls the body's release of oxytocin, a neuropeptide, throughout the body to many organs, including the heart.

The brain signals the release of oxytocin during hugging and pleasant physical touch. Oxytocin is released in mother and child during breast-feeding and physiologically creates a calm atmosphere that facilitates mother/infant bonding. Oxytocin reduces the activation of brain circuits involved in fear, increases levels of confidence, and increases both feelings of trust and generosity. Touching and the resulting release of oxytocin also reduce the stress hormone cortisol and buffer the physiological effects of stress reactions.

...children psychologically attach to those who care for them in order to find safety and security. The innate biological drive to seek closeness to a caregiver when we believe we are in danger activates attachment - that is, bonding in both the child and the caregiver. The quality of safety, comfort, protection, and security that is offered to the infant influences the level of trust that develops in her for the rest of her life...Attachment, in psychology, refers to our natural desire for physical and emotional closeness to another person. It happens through engaging with one another and responding to one another. Attachment does not mean possessiveness or control but rather engagement and responsiveness by showing the five A's [attention, appreciation, affection, acceptance and allowing independence]....People who felt secure in childhood have gained stability. This quality makes it possible to state their needs and to ask for resources of

fulfillment from others. (David Richo, *Daring to Trust*, pps. 33-35)

Without the warmth created by a holding environment where these needs are met, the development of the newborn is at risk on many levels. And when these basic needs are not met in early childhood, the adult the child is to become will have a lot of work on herself to do, possibly many years of visits to the therapist, to try and overcome these gaps in her soul.

Development of Self Consciousness

In the spiritual world before birth we experience complete connectedness, this still is the experience at birth. The newborn child experiences a gradual closing off to spirit over several years. William Wordsworth described this in his poem entitled *Intimations of Immortality* that begins:

> *Our birth is but a sleep and a forgetting*
> *The soul that rises with us, our life's star*
> *Hath had elsewhere its setting*
> *And cometh from afar*
> *Not in entire forgetfulness*
> *And not in utter nakedness,*
> *But trailing clouds of glory do we come*
> *From God, who is our home*
> *Heaven lies about us in our infancy.*

Little by little we start to experience *self* as separate from all that is *other* until eventually we are deep in the loneliness of isolation, of separateness. By the time of his mid 30's, he may have feelings of isolation and deep separateness. He fully experiences the fragmentation of the physical and social world. Family situations, a spouse, a job, or a community are not mitigating factors. It is an inner, personal experience of aloneness. Out of our own will and thinking forces, and out of our own choosing (it is not a given) we can take up a path, a spiritual practice that can recreate feelings of connectedness. This is the central element of all spiritual tradition, to become connected to self and spirit. And this is the path of being human, the path of becoming truly human. For the adult it becomes a path of connecting with the pure joy of our core being that we may have lost touch with since our early years. We take up a path of self development to re-attain the feelings of connection to others and the world, to have some echoes of the joy of spiritual life that was experienced before birth. This is the experience of being human.

During the first seven years, there are two processes at work on the child; the development of the physical body, and the increasing consciousness of self as an experiential reality.

Before birth, the child's entire world is the mother's womb. Sounds and light and temperature are moderated by the mother's body. The child's world is quiet, watery, warm and dark. Birth is a sort of traumatic experience – the child is squeezed through a narrow space distorting his shape, and comes into a world that is cold, bright, dry and loud by comparison. The newborn baby is bathed in a multitude of new experiences, colors and shapes, sounds, smells and tastes, temperature variations and more. All sense experiences are perceived by this being who as yet has no capacity for adding concept and relationship to the sensations. At this stage life is experience without awareness of self, and without cognizing that the thing creating the sensation is somehow separate from himself. The newborn lives fully in the world of the experiences and is not separate from them. His consciousness is completely in his experiences, in his perceptions.

...to know the human being you must contemplate him from three points of view... You can only handle it [spirit] rightly if you treat of conditions of consciousness. The spirit must be grasped by

means of conditions of consciousness such as sleeping and waking. (R. Steiner, *Study of Man*, p. 123)

With the limbs it is different again. Here, from the first moment of life spirit, soul and body are intimately connected; they all flow into one another. Moreover it is here that the child is first fully awake, as those who have to bring up these lively, kicking little creatures in their babyhood very well know. Everything is awake but absolutely unformed. This is the great secret of man: when he is born his head spirit is already highly developed, but asleep. His head soul, when he is born, is very highly developed, but it only dreams. The spirit and soul have yet to gradually awaken. The limb man is indeed fully awake at birth, but unformed, undeveloped. (R. Steiner, Study of Man, p.151

The infant is asleep in terms of any conscious awareness of self. There is a gradual waking up over years, becoming a dreamlike experience for much of early childhood. And then, hopefully, in adulthood, there is a contained-within, full experience of awakeness. I am a self, I am in the center of my world of experience. This physical form contains me within the boundaries of my skin, and I am interacting with what is around me.

A newborn does not yet experience himself as a separate self contained within a body. All of the sensations he experiences are pure sense impressions with no concepts or judgment attached. All experience is part of experience, not separated into *me* and *not me*. All experiences are new and full of amazement and wonder for the child. He does not have a concept of, 'That is mommy, this is me.' He does not think, 'I am here, and blanket is on me.' During the early years of life each sensory experience is a part of developing a living experience of the self. One task for parents and teachers is the creating of an environment that provides nurturing sensory experience for the child. This is the raw data the child's developing self-awareness is founded upon, and is especially significant during the first one or two years of life. The young child is fully a sense organ, taking in all levels of experience as the substance with which it is developing its physical body and its soul character. All the senses are active in delivering sensation, or information, to the young child who has openness to his whole environment. The child has a total trust in the world he has chosen to enter, and the human beings whom he meets. He drinks it all in with awe and wonder and amazement. One can say the consciousness of the infant is all around him in the periphery, not in his center. *All is one*, everything is connected, in the infant's experience.

One day, perhaps at three months old, while lying on his back a shape floats past his eyes, perceived as a visual image. He does not name it *hand*, nor *my hand*. It is simply shape, color, and movement. Then one time, he does something or other, and the observed item ("hand") moves. He tries it again and again and is more and more able to make the thing do stuff. One day there are two similar objects "hands") floating around his field of vision. They touch each other. He feels the touch. This is a major moment because baby has found himself. He finds the boundary of his physical body – his skin. As he becomes more able to control the hand, he aims it, tries to grasp items, pull them in toward mouth. He comes to sitting up, standing, walking away from mommy and daddy; all little steps towards the awareness of self. One pre-school at the beginning of their school year had name tags on their backs of the two- and three-year-old children so as they were walking/running the other way from the teachers, their names were visible.

He is beginning to make speech sounds and to imitate language, to try it out; first sounding, then naming, and then putting phrases together, trying out grammar and syntax. It is a common phrase for a toddler, while reaching his hands upwards toward the adult, "Pick you up." Soon he starts to call himself by his name, "Bobby want drink." And perhaps around two-and-a-half or three years old, 'Me want" turns into 'I want." Little by little there is a waking up process is taking it own course. Painful experiences are bigger and more rapid jumps toward self awareness; pain wakes children up into their own bodies. In fact, for many adults, the earliest memories that can be recalled are painful ones.

During these early years the young child has a need for repetition of all experiences; "Again,…again….and again…" Three and four year olds ask for the same story over and over. As we will discuss later in this chapter, repetition serves a neurological developmental need. Repetition also serves as a will building and strengthening activity. Adults need to be aware of this and support the child's desire for having the same things over and again, because it is serves a developmental need.

Along with the awakening of the sense of self is the arising of the intellect, little by little. The intellect is a human thinking faculty that observes and makes judgments. While the youngest children are fully engaged in their experiences, as the intellect arises, there is a separation from the experience to a place of thinking about it, conceptualizing it, observing it. The intellect acts like the *self* from which everything else is *other*. It is a powerful tool for thinking, and it is a force creating the experience of separateness.

A particular developmental stage is named the 'terrible twos' because at that age, often the child is saying 'No!' to just about everything coming from his parents. This is thought of as a 'terrible' time. When considered rightly, it is a time of incredible strides toward an awareness of self in the young child. He is saying, "No. That is not me." "No. That also is not me." "Yes. THIS is me." "No. No. No. Not me, not me, not me." Him saying 'No' to you means 'yes' to self.As the child moves into and past toddlerhood, the sleeping consciousness turns into a dream-like experiencing of the self, and gradually leads to a waking experience of the adult. So that by age 21 it is possible that the core essence of our selves, our spirit I, begins to be accessible to us. Is the I of the human being not present until age 21? No, we are just not conscious of it, not yet connected to it. The I is at work throughout early childhood building and transforming the physical body with the activity of the etheric body.

Jaimen MacMillan, director of the Spatial Studies Institute, pointed to an accelerating effects to the awakening experience of self common to many families in the modern world. So many little children are shown photos and videos of themselves while they are still a young child. The parent says, "Who's that? That's you." "Who's that baby? You." Jaimen says the less young children view photos of themselves the better – it brings them the idea that who they are is their body – this seeing of themselves wakes them prematurely into experiencing the body as self. Now, when digital cameras and phones that take photos are everywhere, and the photos are instantly able to be displayed, as soon as the photo or video is taken, the children say, "Let me see. Let me see."

There were no mirrors in my Nana's house.
And the beauty that I saw in everything was in her eyes.
I never knew that my skin was too black.
I never knew that my nose was too flat.
I never knew that my clothes didn't fit.
I never knew there were things that I'd missed,
'Cause the beauty in everything was in her eyes.
The world outside was a magical place.
I only knew love.
I never knew hate.
And the beauty in everything was in her eyes.
(excerpt from the song *No Mirrors in My Nana's House*, by Ysaye Barnwell, 1992

Many childhood games and rhymes echo the self-development process the children are engaged in. They give pictures of this process of the I incarnating from the spiritual world into a physical body. Examples include; *Humpty Dumpty*, *Ring a ring a Roses*, and *Jack and Jill*. The young child like to climb up, and jump down from everything available – over and over and over. These games and activities are a reflection of the child coming to earth, to physical reality.

In this process if incarnating, of coming 'down' to earth, the human being undergoes a gradual separating, a loss of connection from spirit beings, from nature and cosmos, and from human beings. There also is a gradual loss of the capacity to perceive nature forces at work directly.

Matthew, a 5-year-old boy in my kindergarten, was a very serious fellow. He did not engage in the jokes and tricks played by his peers. He was quiet, and seemed very thoughtful for a young boy. One day in our play yard he went over to one of the apple trees. There was a hole in the trunk. Matthew put his ear over the hole, and stood there for a couple of minutes, for five minutes, and still was there when my colleague went over to him.

"Matthew, what are you doing?"
"Shhhhhh! I'm listening.

She was surprised, and after a minute or two,
"What are you listening to?
"I hear them working in there. Shhh."
I have no doubt that he was hearing something. Later, when the children went home, I went over for a listen. Nothing.

Young children are able to experience levels of reality that are not accessible for most adults. Matthew was hearing or sensing in some way the working of the elemental beings, the elemental forces of nature. Many children speak of the various beings they observe in nature. Grown-ups think a lot, and anthropomorphize thereby re-describing these beings as little people looking creatures with wings, on little people-like beings with pointy shoes and big hats. Children see directly the etheric forces at work in nature.

There have been countless times when I have been thinking about something, and a child will say something to me as if they were in on my inner thinking process. This is so common an experience for teachers and parents, and it is simply that children's sense capacity includes sensing thoughts. The arising of the intellect and awareness of the self as a separate being from all that is around it leads to a gradual diminishing of the faculty of sensing thoughts and feelings of others, and a loss of the direct experience of forces of nature.

Physical Development

Turning now to physiological development, we first notice the newborn has a head that is proportionally large, approximately one quarter of her entire length. There is a saying that children grow from the head down, and this is due to the body having to 'catch up' to the head in size. An adult has a head approximately one eighth of the total body height.

One of the important tasks for the young child is the development of their own body. The organs at birth are not mature in either form or function and the development of those organs requires much of the child's energy and life forces, though in an unconscious way of course. For this development to unfold properly, the child needs a safe environment that surrounds it with soul and physical warmth. At birth, the senses are ready to be active in receiving sense impressions from the baby's environment. Smell and taste are immediately active. Baby's sense of touch is also well developed at birth; the receptors are located all over the body – the skin. Receptors in the skin also register warmth. The newborn already is able to observe contours and shapes amongst the various visual sensations they receive, though the visual images are not fully focused yet. The baby can distinguish human voices from other sound sources. At birth, the inner ear is practically mature; it is fully functional for receiving auditory signal and sending it to the brain. Over the first few months, the sensory systems develop quickly giving more detail and discrimination to the infant in all his senses. This increase in sense experiencing stimulates a particular part of the brainstem which in turn releases neurotransmitters that make baby more alert, and more interested in new sense experiences.

Sense organs are throughout the body, but the center of the nerve system which processes them is centered in the head, the brain, which in the young child is developing, and being developed based on the sensation received. A baby's brain is only partially developed at birth.

A full-term baby comes into the world with billions of neurons which have to form quadrillions of connections to function effectively. In response to stimuli from the environment through the sense organs (for example, eyes, ears, nose, tongue, skin, muscle joints), the neurons in the relevant part of the brain form connections – synapses - that allow the brain to recognize the signals sent to it from the sense organs via the neural pathways. There is an intensive spurt in production of synapses and neural pathways during the first three years of life, gradually decreasing until age 10 or so, though some functional brain development extends into the mid- or late-twenties. This is the 'wiring' of the brain. At the same time that the brain is being wired in this early period of development, there is an important process of pruning away neurons, synapses and even entire neural pathways that are not being stimulated. Those that are not used or are not efficient pathways are eliminated. Every response to sense impressions such as sight, sound, feelings, etc... makes more neural connections. Repetition is a key element in neurological development, in the development of neural pathways and their myelination. There is a faint neural path at first, through repetition it becomes more distinct, and then becomes covered with an insulating sheath of myelin. Myelination makes for processing efficiency. Myelin is a fatty sheath that insulates the long, tentacle-like axons of nerve cells, enhancing their ability to conduct electrical signals. What is in the environment of the young child - objects, people and their words, moods, thoughts, temperature, etc... - is actually what is forming their organs, and shaping their developing soul forces...all coming through the doorway of the senses.

When some kind of [sensory] *stimulus activates a neural pathway, all the synapses that form that pathway receive and store a chemical signal. Repeated activation increases the strength of that signal. When the signal reaches a threshold level (which differs for different parts of the brain) something extraordinary happens to that synapse. It becomes exempt from elimination - and retains its protected status into adulthood. Scientists do not yet fully understand the mechanism by which this occurs; they conjecture that the electrical activity produced when neural pathways are activated gives rise to chemical changes that stabilize the synapse.* (Rima Shore, *Rethinking the Brain* from the Families and Work Institute in the United States)

At birth infants' brains recognize differences in speech sounds. Until about six months, babies detect differences in sounds from languages other than their mother tongue. By 12 months or so, they have lost this capacity and are most sensitive to the sounds of the language spoken in their immediate environment, the language in their family. Speech sounds in the environment heard by child form the very physical organs for hearing speech.By five months or so, babies' sensory systems are effectively connected and work together efficiently. As the child's thinking and memory are developing, an underlying development is occurring in the brain. The different areas of the child's brain are more and more in communication with each other, more and more connected by neural pathways. Brain activity, electrical activity along the neural pathways causes myelination. More brain activity leads to more myelination. More myelin increases brain activity and capacity.

Walking, Speaking and Thinking

Starting before birth, the baby is engaged in random physical movements, not under his conscious control. These randomly generated movements continue after birth, and are often repeated and repeated. This repetition gradually develops neural pathways which gradually develop the functioning in the brain that is able to control movement, a so-called movement center. Paradoxically, random movement leads to brain development which is then able to control movement.

As the infant is engaged in all the various movement activities of developing balance, sitting up, crawling, standing, walking, etc...he is developing the capacity for speaking because it is these movements which are developing the neurology that will be more able to control finer and finer motor activities, including speaking. Speaking is an array of motor activities including tongue, mouth, larynx, and lungs.

Out of speech develops the beginnings of thinking – thinking is in words….The more the child develops their sense of movement and a capacity for flexibility of movement, later they will be able to be flexible in their thinking and move with the ideas of others. The more the child refines his movement capacities and abilities, he defines his physical body and develops physical skills. During the first several years of life three profound human tasks are being accomplished by the young child, the development of the capacities for walking, speaking and thinking. All of these activities are learned out of the inner drive of the child yet cannot occur without the example of other human beings engaged in them. These three capacities to a large degree define what it is to be human. Walking, speaking and thinking are three activities of the human I, though not taken up in self consciousness. There is an unconscious impulse toward the upright position, the vertical - the child needs the example of human uprightness. His will is active without fear in developing this upright capacity. Learning to speak requires speaking human beings for imitation. The vocal organs and hearing system are formed by sounds of the mother tongue spoken in infant's environment. Thinking is founded on the development of speaking because most human beings think in words, not images.

Until the change of teeth, the child is definitely dependent on imitation for learning what is taught. What you demonstrate to the child works like an outer stimulus that calls upon the child's entire bodily organization – in some places more visibly, in others less visibly – to imitate the impression. To substantiate this, we need only keep in mind the decisive fact that children acquire their native language wholly through imitation, which works deeply into the organization of their bodies and souls. We must take into account that the vibration, the waves of movement, of any spoken sound is experienced much more intensely in childhood that it is later in life. Even in speaking, when it is a person's native language that is in question, any adjusting of the larynx, any inner ensouling of the organs, is based on imitation....Consider how close the child's soul life, which arises out of this imitative activity, is to the life of the parents simply because the child is a being who imitates. If we really grasp how strong the tendency toward imitation is in the child, we have to come to a holy awe and a profound respect for the child/parent relationship. (R. Steiner, *Rudolf Steiner in the Waldorf School,* 6/1/1924, p. 213-214)

In the very young baby can be seen basic instincts that come purely from the physical body, and they are similar to instincts in animals. These instincts are exhibited as movement patterns, reflexes. By three or four months, instinct diminishes as a driving force and the developing baby is now guided by its I-being active with its will as it responds in imitation. For example, animals learn to stand and walk without an example to imitate. They develop this purely out of instinct. A human baby needs to imitate a walking person to develop standing and walking.

Walking, speaking and thinking are archetypal and unique to the human being, and the style that each individual exhibits toward developing them can be seen as a glimpse of the essence of their soul activity during their life time. How one attains uprightness and walking, for instance, can be seen as *the* gesture of the archetype of the person's biography in this earth life.

It is essential for a growing confidence in himself that the child is the one that achieves these on his own. It is out of the engagement of the will forces by the I, and the accomplishing these very human capacities for him self that a strong self of self arises. Emi Pikler, an MD from Hungary specializing in infant care and education, studied motor development in infants. She spoke extensively about the importance of allowing the child to sit up on their own, when he is able to stand only when he pulls themselves up - to take those first steps out of his own initiative, and solo.

Children who have reached the stages of sitting and walking on their own initiative, through their own independent efforts, move more steadily, less spasmodically, with more adroitness and harmony than do other children. (Emi Pikler, *Some Contributions to the Study of the Gross Motor Development of Children, Journal of Genetic Psychology*, 1968, p. 37)

Pikler's philosophy has been continued in Los Angeles with the work of *Resources for Infant Educarers*. A baby walker for a child not yet able to stand and walk does not enhance or stimulate the development of standing and walking. It is a premature placement of the child in positions they have as yet not attained for themselves, and may even subtly inhibit his developing sense of self confidence. Throughout life, it is self learned skills that go far deeper into the organization of the one who is learning. So one can consider what sort of environment can be created to foster the learning that would support the particular developmental stages of the child.

Infants have various patterns of movement, or reflexes, that are hard-wired into their neurology and that serve developmental functions. The sucking reflex, grasping reflex, tonic neck reflexes and so on are patterns of movement that must become integrated into the functioning of the body so that individual parts of the body by age seven can operate freely, without the participation of other parts. The overcoming of these reflex patterns comes though the normal movement developmental stages of rolling, crawling, standing, and walking, though sometimes additional support is needed. In our times of extensive time spent traveling in vehicles wherein the child is seated in a safety restraint device, and significant time spent immobile, time spent in baby-walker/ bouncers before the baby can even sit up or stand, and the passive experiencing of on-screen entertainment, these patterned movements seem to stick around longer in more and more children. The child needs to be in movement and in direct connection to the sources of sensory stimulation with all senses active and engaged. The flexibility and capacity for movement in the young child has a direct correlation to the movement of imagination and thinking capacities in the adult. During the entire first six or seven years, the child is refining his movement capacities as a foundation for his later life.

Etheric Activity

If one considers the activities of the formative aspect of the etheric forces, it is clear that they are most active around the head for the first two years or so. Brain development predominates, and the nervous and sensory systems are being enhanced. Then until age four or five, the formative focus is on the trunk and the organs within, especially the rhythmic system involving heart and lungs. In the last years of early childhood, until approximately age 7, the etheric body is most active in the limbs and the digestive/metabolic system.

This is visible; we see at birth the large head, then from two to four a major growth spurt in the trunk. And by age six the limbs have become long and gangly and the child often is knocking things over and bumping into people and things with their newly lengthened limbs. This is a way to track visually the activity and movement of the child's etheric forces. And it is a way to know when those forces are freed to be available for new types of memory activities and academic beginnings. When those etheric forces are freed from their bodily-forming activities is also the time when one can begin to see the arising of the child's temperament which is an interaction between their particular physical body and their own etheric body. The first seven years of life is the time of greatest growth in height and weight, a major period of brain development, of sense organ development, in fact the whole nervous system. The heart and lungs take a bit longer, and the skeletal system still longer. But by age seven the etheric formative forces have done their major formative work and are now metamorphosing into forces of intellect for thinking and new memory activities.

One can observe a vast intelligence at work in the building of the body and perfecting its functioning which cannot be explained simply by DNA activity. This intelligence has a task during the first seven years to build a body suitable for earthly life, a nearly miraculous task. As the body is more and more formed, this intelligence becomes available for other activities that call for intelligence such as newly acquired types of thinking in the child. One cannot go back and rebuild the organs later in life, so adults are responsible for creating an environment where the child's formative etheric forces are left free to work on body development until they show they are done. Then we can say the etheric body is born, and that is not until six or seven years of age.

There are a number of visible physical signs announcing the ending of the early childhood years. They include the appearance of arches in the feet, the thinning down of fingers so that knuckles become visible, loss of baby fat so that pants require belts or suspenders, the lengthening of the limbs and the pushing out of the baby teeth by the permanent ones. These are signs that say, 'Now the formative forces of the etheric body are available for new thinking activities.'

A major task during the first seven years is to spiritualize matter – the spirit transforms the hereditary physical body into what it needs to live within. This is accomplished by the *I* directing the formative activity of the etheric body, but totally below the radar of the child's awareness. The maintenance aspects of the etheric body are self-sustaining, they function automatically and autonomously.

Imitation and the Senses

What creates the personality or soul of the human being? Often it is attributed to either nature or nurture, but it is not an either/or situation. It is *both and*. Nature and nurture and the I being are the threefold aspects active in the developing human being. A person is an I being born into a hereditary body, trying to form and take hold of it as it grows and develops in its particular surroundings and environment.

What I have been describing to you...is the true human being, the human being that is an instrument for perceiving the world, for experiencing it through the soul and grasping it spiritually. That is the true human being. And what the human being is actually forms the physical body. I have not been describing human beings in a finished condition but rather what is active in them. All that activity, everything that works together in the physical, soul, and spiritual planes, is what forms human beings as they stand upon this planet. (R. Steiner, *A Psychology of Body, Soul and Spirit*, p. 41)

It is through the senses that one relates to the world around them as well as relating to other human beings. All sense impressions are images that give information to the recipient. The content of sense perception, along with hereditary genetic information are what forms the young child. The child is receiving images of all kinds including images of human activity in their environment, images streaming toward earth from the cosmos and images from the world of nature around them. Human organs are formed and developed out of these received images. We come from the cosmos, and cosmic images form our physical being as well as constitute our life forces. As was mentioned earlier, the human soul is the intermediary between the spirit and the physical aspects of the human being. The soul is the recipient of sense impression – the soul's activity is in response to these sensations, and can take the form of thinking, feeling and willing, or doing, or various combinations of those soul faculties. At various stages in one's life, one or another of these faculties is more prominent. In the first seven years of life, the most prominent soul activity is willing. The newly born human being is trying to grasp the world, to touch it, taste it, move it, move on it, and in general *do* things with it. The information, or images, received as sense impressions are taken into the human organism through the window of the soul faculties of thinking, feeling and willing. Sense perceptions relate us to our surroundings. Young children being primarily will oriented beings, thereby have an impulse toward imitating what they perceive while adults may think about, or feel, or do something in response to a sense experience.

While spirit beings in the spirit world, we live as joy connected to all others in joy. When children are born, they relate to human beings in the same way. What they experience of other human beings is all such a joy, so awe-filled and amazing, that they can only imitate it. It is not thought about, they just imitate out of an inner drive to connect.

Rudolf Steiner described this in young children as a sort of physical religion. Devotion to all other beings in the spiritual world becomes imitation in the physical world. The young child has a love of all things physical, and all things that human beings do in the world.

When I was a child, there was an advertisement on TV paid for by the American Cancer Society. It stands out vividly in my memory, though it was forty years ago. The 30-second piece was in black and white. A father and son (five-ish year old) are walking in the woods. The father looks up at a tree. The boy watches his father look up, and then looks up at the tree. The father looks out over a lake. The boy watches father, and then looks out over lake. Father sits down and leans against a tree. The boy sits down and leans against the tree, just in the same position as the father. Then the father takes out a cigarette and lights it. The boy looks on. Finally, the narrator speaks, "Like father, like son. Think about it." A powerful message because it presents the chilling truth of how young children learn in an amazing 30 second flow of images.

Play has the utmost importance in the development of the young child. For him, there is no difference between work and play. There is however the possibility of total engagement in the activity at hand. From taking the pots and pans from the cupboard and tossing them to the floor, to pushing a small wooden car, to 'pretending' he is a pilot to using a piece of wood and naming it his violin - all varieties of play are the essential avenue by which the young child comes to grasp the physical and social worlds.

Part pure experimentation and part imitation, this is how the young child learns. It is our responsibility as adults to create an environment in which the child can play.

Play gives children a chance to practice what they are learning...They have to play with what they know to be true in order to find out more, and then they can use what they learn in new forms of play. (the late Fred Rogers of Mister Rogers' Neighborhood)

The young child is a will being - through his will, he grasps reality. In his play, will, feeling and thinking are united. Subject and object are as one for him. From a physiological development point of view, play reinforces neural connections, and lack of play results in fewer neural connections. For young children play, not instruction, is what makes the greatest impact on brain development. A baby's brain is only partially developed at birth. Trillions of nerve cells or neurons are developed just prior to birth, but these neurons are not connected. The development of a person's brain happens most rapidly during the first three years of life as connections, or synapses, are developed between neurons. It is the development of these synapses that forms a person's capacity for intelligence. The period of the first three years of life is critical because after developing synapses the brain goes through a process of pruning away or eliminating the neural connections that are not frequently used. Synapses are formed through nurturing verbal, auditory and tactile activity. Early experience has a dramatic impact on the brain wiring process.

Listening to adults speak or listening to and watching electronic screens does not nurture growth of neural connections. The activities that most effectively develops neural connections are direct interaction between adults and children, and in play interactions between children and children. In play activities children can develop capacities in multiple domains. Verbal, conceptual, motor, emotional, psychological and creative capacities can all be developed through natural playful activities.

When the child is born, he is not able to direct his body yet. So the first learning is a becoming able to operate the vehicle he is born into. When he has developed a beginning awareness of self and some capacity for self-directed movement, the next step is learning how to care for his body. The realm of hygiene includes using the toilet, washing his hands and body, only putting edible items into his mouth, and wiping his own nose and bottom. The next level is learning to help take care of the home and garden. For a young child, their home is an extension of the body, and learning to care for it is important. He can sweep, and fold laundry, set the table for meals, wipe the table and take out the compost. All of these skills are learned through imitation, the primary learning tool of early childhood. It is a like a series of concentric circles with the child at the center, then bodily hygiene activities around him, surrounded by house and garden care, and finally out into the world around him. When the child is ready, he looks out over the fence in the garden and wonders what is out there. The formative life forces have done the majority of their work and are freed for something new. It is time for something new. Grade school is around the corner and a new style of learning is on its way. Soon, instruction will become the key to teaching him.

Some guidelines to consider

1. Allow enough time for free play - without adult intervention and interruption (adult's eyes open, mouth closed)

2. Provide suitable play areas/environment

3. Provide suitable toys – simple things that allow the child to 'complete' with his own imagination.

4. Contact with world of nature – the four elements as well as natural settings.

5. Provide examples of the adult doing real work - the true engaged will of adult.

6. Provide artistic activities and supplies that allow child to freely express what is within them.

7. Provide nourishing images from stories and circle time.

Play is essential to a child's development. Everything is learned through play

Chapter 3

The Senses as Doorways of Relating

*Our sense perceptions provide the basis for
the rest of our soul life.*
Rudolf Steiner
Anthroposophy (A Fragment), p. 98

Now, this means that the first three years of life are those which prepare the child to become a member of the humanity. Man is born out of the isolation in which he existed in the maternal womb, because there he was nothing else but an isolated, developing being; a being given up to cosmic powers; a being spun into its own karma. This however is a germ which unfolds and grows into walking, into speaking and communicating, and into thinking and imparting, thereby developing the prerequisites for a social life... We also know that something else develops out of walking, speaking and thinking. The sense of word develops out of walking and thereby speaking comes into being; the sense of thought develops out of speaking and thereby thinking emerges, while the sense of Ego develops out of thinking and thereby the knowledge, the immediate sensory experience arises that the other person is an individual. You see, walking, speaking and thinking are the prerequisites for a social organism. (Karl Konig, *Man As A Social Being and the Mission of Conscience* pps. 38-39)

Sense organs are communication links between the organism and the world around. Through the senses we receive images, or information, by which we learn to relate to ourselves, the world around us and each other. The senses are providing the information by which the *I* is able to be active and engage. Human beings perceive and experience the world through the sense organs.

The information, or images, received as sense impressions are taken into the human organism through the window of the soul leading to responses and/or reactions in thinking, feeling and/or willing.

Let me put it this way: we are here; the world is outside us. We perceive this world, we take in what it has to give us, as it were, and we continue to carry this in our soul as we go about the world. The objects are outside us, the beings are outside us, and

what they impart to us through our perception of them we carry
with us in our soul. [as mental picture, as memory.] (R. Steiner,
The Realm of Language, Dornach, 7/17/1915, p. 1

Young children being primarily will-oriented beings thereby have
an impulse toward imitating what they perceive, to do what they
see. Adults may think about, or feel, or do something in response
to a sense experience.

Adult bodies and souls are already formed, but young children
are in a process of forming their bodies and developing soul
response patterns that are affected by all of their experiences.
Sensory experiences are part of what is forming them. The I
interacts with the world through its own soul, and it is the soul
and body that sense impressions imprint upon. Also at work are
other levels of sense experience, not noticeable by most adults.
Children before age seven directly experience the moods,
feelings and thoughts of the adults in their environment. The
young child is wholly a sense organ, quite a bit like a sponge,
soaking in all levels of experience into the process of forming
their physical body and their soul life.

All of these experiences, all of the sense perceptions and non-
sensory awareness (of feelings and thoughts) relate to the
developing child as formative qualities. The child receives
myriad images from the natural world around him, from human
adults in his world, and even in the light streaming towards him
from the stars and planets, all as substance for his formative
forces to utilize in forming the organs, and creating patterns of
soul and personality.

It is important to consider the source of the images received by
the child. Are the images healthy for a developing being? Are the
images truthful and following laws of nature and cosmos? Are
they images electronically created and crafted to create
consumers? Adults have the responsibility for the environment in

which the child is immersed, as part of guiding the young child into the world. A consideration of what images we want for our developing child, and what is the source of those images must be part of our awareness.

There are at least twelve senses that are conduits for receiving images and perceptions of various kinds. It is through the senses that one relates to the world around them as well as relating to human beings. All sense impressions are images of a kind, touch, sound, taste all are received by the human being as an image. One could say it is images that form the young child, that form the human being; images of all kinds including images of human activity in their environment, images streaming toward earth from the cosmos and images from the world of nature around us. Human organs are formed and developed out of images received from the cosmos and from the human beings around them. We come from the cosmos, and cosmic images form our physical being and constitute our life forces.

The etheric body which develops in the human being is a world in itself. One might say that it is a universe in the form of images…It is of extraordinary significance that we, in our descent into earthly life, draw together forces from the universal ether and thus take with us, in our ether body, a kind of image of the cosmos. If one could extract the ether body of a person at the moment when he is uniting himself with the physical body, we should have a sphere which is far more beautiful than any formed by mechanical means – a sphere containing stars, zodiac, sun and moon. These configurations of the ether body remain during embryonic development, while the human being grows together more and more with his physical body…Indeed they remain right into the seventh year, until the change of teeth. (Steiner, May 26, 1922, Dornach)

Steiner described the life senses, or the lower senses, as those that give experiences of one's own body. Through the sense of **Touch** one experiences one's own limits. The sense receptors are the skin, the covering around our entire body. We usually are not aware of our sense of **Life** because it is a general feeling of well-being, of physical harmony. We only experience this sensing when our life processes are out of balance, as sensed by the body's inner organs. Then we feel out of sorts and ill at ease. This sense is connected to how well one is nourished by rest, nutrition and immune system health.

Dr. Susan Johnson (www.youandyourrchildshealth.org) describes the function of the sense of life as determining whether to tell the bodily organism to be dominated by the parasympathetic nervous system or the sympathetic system. The sympathetic system is active when there is stress on the system, whether it is food that cannot be digested or anxiety due to others' behavior, and makes the body ready for fight or flight reactions, as well as inhibiting digestion. The parasympathetic system can be called the rest and digest system, creating feelings of safety calm, and allowing the body to be relaxed and take in experiences in a manner that feels safe and can be digested. We as the adults have to create an environment without stress where the child can can function from the relaxed place of their parasympathetic nervous system.

The sense of **Self Movement** is how we experience our own body moving in space and nerve cells in the muscles and joints are the sense organs, and how freely we move through space. The sense of **Balance** is both the equilibrium of the body in space, as well as inner balance and calm. The physical organ that senses balance is the inner ear. These four lower senses deliver the relationship of self to body.

It is vitally important to support the development of these four life senses on the young child. Babies need to experience loving, warm touch. They need to be held and cuddled. We need to be aware of how much touch any particular child needs; some have difficulty with the same type of touch that others enjoy. There are 'touch-sensitive' children and we have to support them in getting the particular kinds of touch they need. Many babies and young children are calmed by gentle foot squeezing and massage, though for some their feet are too sensitive and ticklish. A life of daily rhythms supports the developing life sense in the young child. Regular meal times and sleeping times including napping (read *The 7 O'Clock Bedtime: Early to bed, early to rise, makes a child healthy, playful, and wise* by Inda Schaenen.) Calmness at mealtimes is a also big help.

Young children need the opportunity to move freely! Activities involving free exploration of nature, and climbing, and rolling all support the developing sense of movement. Bodily experiences of freedom are the basis for the possibility of the free human being. Hindrances in this development include time spent in car seats, time in baby walkers and bouncers at a time when they are still unable to stand or walk, and time spent in front of electronic screen entertainments.

The developing sense of balance is also aided by rolling and climbing, also spinning round and round. Walking on narrow surfaces such as balance beams, and hopping from one step to another are examples of balance development activities.

Through the senses of **Smell, Taste, Sight,** and **Warmth** the human being brings some of the world into itself and becomes aware of their relation to the world. These 'middle' senses bring awareness of the relationships of the self to the world around. Warmth is both physical and soul temperature and is sensed *in relation to* one's own warmth. Warmth perception stimulates the human being to warm or cool himself to the degree necessary to meet the other.

The higher senses relate the self to other human beings, and can be considered the spiritual senses. Through these senses we find our connection to other human beings. The four higher senses develop out of the foundation of the life senses. Each of the life senses supports the development of a particular higher sense as the individual grows and matures throughout life. The life senses give information about the human being's own body while the same function turned outwards gives similar information yet it is about another person, not one's self. The lower senses turned outwards are higher, spiritual senses, delivering information about the other the human being with whom we are interacting. In a sense, when one is receiving information through the higher senses, it is out-of-body experience.

The child's sense of balance, whose sense organ is the inner ear, is a foundation for the sense of **Hearing** the other – not the words, but the way the words are used, the musicality of sound and tone. Through this we experience not the content, but the intent of the words we hear spoken. Young children understand the meaning of what is spoken through their sensing tone, long before they understand the words of a language. Hearing is the only one of the higher senses that is based in a physical organ. Hearing the other requires an inner stillness and calm, an inner quiet, so that sound sensations can be received.

The sense of our own body's movement through space supports a sense for the **Speech**, or **Word**, of the other. Through this sense one gets an experience of how the words of another human being move. And to understand another's ideas we must hear them expressed as words. When one has freedom and flexibility of movement, it is easier to move along with the spoken words of another person.

The sense of life, an inner sense of one's general physical harmony and well-being, is needed for a sense for the **Idea**, or the **Concept**, of the other. This is how one can experience the thinking of another human being. What is the idea this person is trying to express? Just as the sense of life is a sort of gauge for etheric balance, the sense of thought of the other is also a sensing of the etheric world, the world where thinking lives. We relate to each other in understanding by means of the thinking which is revealed in speech. Hearing, Word and Idea senses work together when, for instance, one wonders; 'What I hear you saying is this. Is this what you mean? Is this the idea you are trying to convey?'

The sense of touch is the other end of the spectrum of the sense of the **Ego of the other.** A developed sense of physical touch underlies the capacity to touch the very being of another individual human being whom one meets and experiences.

The perception of another human being is image sensation; as actuality, stands the fulfillment of what the sense of touch gives, so that, in this inwardness, the reality is given wherein the sense of touch is grounded. (Steiner, *Anthroposophy (A Fragment)*, p. 203)

The ability to sense the Ego of another is based on a confidence in one's own awareness of self. 'I can let you into my inner life, because I trust in my awareness of who I am.'

Man as far as he is at rest, as far as he is the motionless human figure which has so to speak the head at its center, is the organ of perception for the Ego of the other human being is the biggest organ of perception which we have and we ourselves are as physical man the biggest organ of perception which we have. (R. Steiner, *Das Ratsel des Menschen. Die Geistegen Hintergrunde dermenschlichen Geschichte,* from Karl Konig, *Man As A Social Being and the Mission of Conscience,* p. 137)

The sense of Ego of the Other works in sleeping and waking – we 'fall asleep,' in a sense, into the other, and then immediately reawaken back in ourselves. This is a sort of higher breathing process which works in a matter of seconds only. (see chapter 5) Empathy is based on sensing the other, and falling asleep to one's self.

Another way to think about Steiner's depiction of twelve senses is to consider them as eight senses. There are the four middle senses of Smell, Taste, Sight, and Warmth, and there are but four other senses. These other four have both an inward aspect and an outward aspect. They are Touch/Ego, Life/Idea, Movement/Word and Balance/Hearing. Any way you delineate the senses, they are the conduits for the images that are the nutrition for the body and soul of the developing child. Through various flows of sensation and information to the human being through the sense organs raw material is received for the building up of body and soul. It is these images that form the developing human, both in his physical form and functioning, as well as his soul constitution.

Are there still higher and lower senses? Yes – those mentioned thus far represent just a partial list. Other senses exist both above and below those we have discussed. (R. Steiner, p. 19, *A Psychology of Body, Soul and Spirit*,10/23/1909)

The healthy development of the life senses, the four 'lower' senses, requires a healthy diet of images so those senses develop to their fullest possibility. Then is in place a sound foundation for the much later development of the higher senses, the capacities for sensing the other. These are truly social senses, and are the basis for understanding and empathy for others. Attention to the development of the senses in young human beings is at the core of an education attempting to renew culture and create a fertile ground for human connecting. These twelve senses are the doorways to relating the self to the body, the self to the world around and the self to other human beings.

The human being has a hunger for sense impressions. (Dennis Klocek, *Knowledge, Teaching and the Death of the Mysteries*, lecture 2) It is because sense impressions form us at a young age and can nourish and rejuvenate us later in life. The modern world is running amok with images. We are bombarded with images from media of all kinds, from electronic screens to billboards and magazines and t-shirts. One can sense a sort of image craving in our world perhaps because the human being is seeking images that are 'healthy' in the midst of so much that is not. Life giving, life affirming images are vitally important for the young child. The development of the senses in the young child, especially the four 'life senses,' is a full time activity. Images, sense experiences of nature, of other human beings, of nutritious and wholesome food are what nourish the young child as they develop their own sense apparatus and the neurological structure to process those sense impressions. Electronically generated images are in fact a hindrance to this development. (see books and articles by Joseph Chilton Pearce, Keith Buzzell, etc...)

We can see the rise of what might be called cultural autism. The symptoms? Tunneled senses, and feelings of isolation and containment. Experience, including physical risk, is narrowing to about the size of a cathode ray tube, or flat panel if you prefer. Atrophy of the senses was occurring long before we came to be bombarded by the latest generation of computers, high-definition TV, and wireless phones.... But the new technology accelerates the phenomenon. "What I see in America today is an almost religious zeal for the technological approach to every facet of life," says Daniel Yankelovich, the veteran public opinion analyst. This faith, he says, transcends mere love for new machines. "It's a value system, a way of thinking, and it can become delusional."
...In The Necessity of Experience [Edward Reed] wrote, "There is something wrong with a society that spends so much money, as well as countless hours of human effort – to make the least dregs of processed information available to everyone everywhere and yet does little or nothing to help us explore the world for ourselves." None of our major institutions or our popular culture pay much notice to what Reed called "primary experience' – that which we can see, feel, taste, hear, or smell for ourselves.
(Richard Louv, *Last Child In the Woods,* p. 64-65*)*

In sensing we have an experience of the thing sensed, the thing generating the sensation, but we do not experience the sensing itself. We only experience that which is creating the sensation. The activity of sensing is below the level of conscious awareness. Young children, through their senses, touch the creator of the thing being sensed. They connect with the creator beings and living concepts that stand behind sense impressions. Images that are filled with life and that come from life nurture and nourish the young child. The child's etheric body and his soul thrive from these life-enriched images, rather than a diet of electronically created images that have no origin in life.

Deep Connecting

By allowing the ego of the other to speak their ideas through their words, by truly entering into their being through deep listening, then our own ego stands naked before them, not judging, but open-hearted and vulnerable. If we can truly stand freed of our me-ness, then our shining ego, truly ready to listen, allows the ego of the other to freely speak. Our ego gives strength to the ego of the other to free itself. The strength arises in being vulnerable and allowing, and then we can experience truly meeting the other.

In the deepening awareness of our own egoism lies the possibility of release from soul reaction patterns or habits ruling our actions. We are freed into connection with our higher ego. Then who meets the other is not our double, but our spiritual core. We then truly live in the realm of the higher senses which is the spiritual world. And our activity allows the other to connect with their ego as well, simply by us being present in that way. We give strength to the other by our allowing what is to just be. We learn to yield to what is. We give away our self, give away our power in freedom and in consciousness, so our spirit-I can guide us. This awake choosing to let go of the self is the path to Love.

Chapter 4

Imitation, Life Activities and the Role of the Adult as Example and Guide

*The task of the kindergarten teacher is to adjust the work
taken from daily life so that it becomes suitable for the children's
play activities. The whole point...is to give
young children the opportunity to imitate to imitate life in a
simple and wholesome way.*
Rudolf Steiner, April 1923

It is not moral preaching and not reasoned instruction that work on children in the right way: that which works is what the adults in their surroundings do visibly before their eyes. - R. Steiner

Imitation is the natural learning mode for the young child. Rudolf Steiner described it as a sort of bodily religion arising from a sense of joy and wonder with all experiences and sensation. The young child, so recently arrived into a physical body from the spiritual world, loves all he meets in the world. The adult, caregiver, kindergarten teacher, parent, etc... has therefore a huge responsibility since the child is molding itself out of its experiences, out of what and who is imitated. Thereby it is incumbent on the adults to create an environment of objects, people and activities that we would be happy to have taken up in imitation by the child. An environment that nurtures the child includes crucial elements that create form and order in the developing child; rhythm in daily life activities, safe and healthy boundaries, and adults' consistency in maintaining the boundaries and rhythm.

A child learns from particular people; depending on its own disposition, he will absorb one or another of their behavioral traits and this in turn will considerably influence his own behavioral patterns and physical functioning. Especially for the young child, *who we are* is what is most imitated and what has the deepest impact on their development in many areas of development. So our attempting to better ourselves has significant impact on the child. Our striving for self-development is worthy of imitating.

The information, or images, received as sense impressions are taken into the child's developing human organism through the window of the soul faculties of thinking, feeling and willing. These sense perceptions relate him to his surroundings. Young children being primarily will oriented beings, thereby have an impulse toward imitating what they perceive while adults may think about, or feel, or do something in response to a sense experience.

During the course of their developmental stages children learn in different ways. In the first years the primary mode of learning is imitation for such diverse behaviors as walking, speaking, eating and hygiene habits, social behaviors such as greeting other people, and so much more. Learning through imitation is teaching yourself according from the example of your perceived role model. Without instruction or cajoling, children take in their experiences of all the events happening in their environment, and are compelled to try them out and practice them out of their own inner drive.

Until this time [the age of six or seven], human beings are fundamentally imitative beings. The constitution of their body and soul is such that they totally devote themselves to their surroundings. They feel their way into the surroundings. They develop themselves from the center of their will so that they mold the force lines and force rays of their will exactly to what occurs in their surroundings. More important than everything that we can bring the child through reprimanding words, through preaching in this stage, is the way we ourselves behave in the presence of the child…In every tone of speech, in every gesture that we as teachers use in the presence of the child during this stage, lies something to which the child adapts itself. As human beings we are much more that we know by the external reflection of our thoughts. In life we pay little attention to how we move a hand, but the way we move a hand is the faithful reflection of the whole state of our souls, the whole reflection of our inner mood. As adults with developed soul lives we pay little attention to the connection between the way we step forward with our legs, the way we gesture with our hands, the expressions on our faces, and the will and feeling impulses that lie in our souls. The child, however, lives in these intangibles. We do not exaggerate when we say that those in the young child's surroundings who inwardly strive to be good, to be moral, who in their thinking and feeling consciously intend to do the child no wrong, even in what is not spoken – such people affect the child in the strongest possible manner through the intangibles of life. (R. Steiner, *The Spirit of the Waldorf School*, p.137)

Children do not learn to stand or walk or speak through instructions or explanation. These human capacities are learned by imitating the examples provided by adults. This concentrated, imitative learning of the child is stimulated by the example of the adult and is tirelessly and fearlessly practiced.

Every education is self-education, and as teachers we can only provide the environment for children's self-education. We have to provide the most favorable conditions where, through our agency, children can educate themselves according to their own destinies. This is the attitude that teachers should have toward children, and such an attitude can be developed only through an ever-growing awareness of this fact. " (Rudolf Steiner, *The Child's Changing Consciousness*)

Young children naturally are most active in the doing, the willing realm of soul life. They are drawn to adults work activity especially when the adult is truly engaged in meaningful working. I experience that when a chair breaks, or we are making lunch, when it is meaningful work that needs to be done, then the older children in kindergarten are attracted to participating and helping, while the younger ones exactly imitate the activities in their play. Young children are drawn to the activities of real workers and crafts people like the blacksmith, the carpenter, spinner, plumber and so on. The experiencing of these activities is a body-building experience for the child, as well as an example of focused adult will for the child's will forces. A young child who experiences and even does various different types of real work is given a blessing of the many images to incorporate into their development.

[His] *body becomes an instrument with all kinds of tones and colors. This is a body the individuality can enter and live in for a lifetime.* (Joop van Dam, *Understanding Imitation Through a Deeper Look at Human Development.* P. 105, in *The Developing Child: The First Seven Years,* WECAN Press)

When the adult fully engages in her own work, the will of the adult is engaged and it is a sort of invitation to the imitative will of the young child. There are certain qualities of this 'real' work for the adult to develop. It is meaningful if you do the work whether or not the children participate. If you are simply doing something so that the children will join in, and then when they don't you put away materials and tools, then clearly it not something important that needs to be done. An essential capacity for the adult to develop is being able to give 100% attention on the work at hand while at the same time giving full attention to what the children are doing. The adult needs eyes and ears in back of head in order to be aware of all the corners of the room or yard. Also, it is an important quality to model that you are planted in one location while focused on the work, rather than a little work, a little roaming the room, a little more work and a little more roaming. This calls for being prepared when you set to the work – all needed tools and materials are at hand, as well as tools and materials for the children who choose to imitate your activity.

There is so much to do to care for a kindergarten home; washing, cooking, sewing, ironing, planting, weeding, pruning, repairing chairs, tables, dolls and other toys, making toys for the kindergarten, and more. Not as activities that are done to give the children projects, but work related to the care and improvement of our kindergarten home.

All learning involves an engagement of the will. Learning requires effort. With young children, the will is directly connected to the sensory activity, without the mediating of thinking or understanding – this is the process of imitation. It is a special art to engage the child's interest and attention that adults must learn. When the adult takes up the tasks that need to be done with joy and with enthusiasm, with their own engaged will, then the child's attention is more likely present on the task as well. Tasks attended to with care and love engage the child's interest much more than tasks done in a disinterested or even resentful way.

One's inner attitude to the work at hand is so important. Do domestic activities conjure thoughts and feelings of drudgery, of chores? If the adult is begrudgingly doing the task, the attitude that the task is unpleasant is passed on to the child. Also, if the adult's heart is not in it, the adult's will is not truly engaged. So the children experience an adult who doesn't want to do it, but is doing it, with just a part of herself involved in the task. Even in the name 'chore' is connotation of something one doesn't want to, but has to do. So consider the language used. 'Task' or 'job' seem to have a nicer ring to them.

At mealtimes, I value sitting at the table through the meal until we are done and getting up together. To teach this practice through imitation, it is incumbent on me to sit down at the table only when everything is set. Serving utensils, bowls, condiments, the food itself, everything that will be needed for the meal has to be set out at the table so that while we are seated together, I don't have to get up for any forgotten items. When the phone rings the answering machine takes care of it. I practice relaxed sitting for the entire mealtime because I am prepared, I have thought ahead. And the children learn through imitation the practice of staying in their seats for the entire meal.

Imitation is not only of behavior and gestures. Imitation is also active in the forming and developing physical body. The organs are actively taking in information via the senses that guide them towards growth of form and functioning. Steiner explained that cosmic wisdom forces are streaming toward the human body, delivering information for physical organ formation. Information also streams toward the young child for the physical and etheric bodies of the adults in their environment. Is liver disease a hereditary function of behavioral traits such as alcoholism being passed on? Or do diseased livers send images of dysfunction to the child's developing liver? I think, *Yes,* and *Yes.*

Young children learn habits of health and hygiene from the adults in their environment. Also learned are the strategies for dealing with challenges and frustration. The reaction patterns of the adults are taken deeply into the child's soul, even as early as the first year, and will consistently reveal themselves over the course of the child's life. Perhaps in adulthood he will visit a counselor and then can begin the work of becoming aware of and transforming these reactive behavior habits he took in as a young child.

Observing young children as they experience music presents a clear picture of their faculty for direct connecting that diminishes as the child gets older. Children under three, upon hearing music, start moving and rocking back and forth – even with no adult dancer to imitate. Very often the three-and-under crowd will spontaneously start 'dancing' to the music, while their parents and most other adults stand quite still, hands in pockets, perhaps secretly tapping a foot. If some adult starts to dance and gives the child attention, the child will smile from ear to ear and continue their 'dancing.' I think the child says to themselves, "Yes! Someone else gets it." The child is directly connecting to the music, it is experienced even into their bones and muscles and the music says '*move your body around.*' The music speaks and the child senses its message directly, with no thinking involved. As the child gets a bit older, perhaps 5 years old, they only seem to dance when there are adults to imitate. By the time of adulthood, self consciousness is so strong that unless one is in an environment where many are dancing, it is the rare individual who is willing to stand out as the only dancing person.

Especially for the young child, the very being of the person is what is most imitated and what has the deepest impact on their development in many areas of development. Our attempting to better ourselves has significant impact on the child. Our striving for self-development is worth imitating. So then the very striving of the adult to develop fuller awareness and new capacities for response penetrates deeply into the developing child and can bear fruit much later in life.

The child regards everything they experience as worthy of imitation and trust. That is why the adult responsibility is so huge, so not to betray this trust.

It is betrayed, however, when the child experiences that an adult does not know his own mind. Likewise, when the course of the day lacks regularity and rhythm and security. But, if good habits are installed in the form of a definite sleeping-waking rhythm, in regular meal times, and regular alternation of play and rest, the child feels herself safe and protected, experiencing the course of such a day as something into which she may gladly enter.

Without such clear and well-formed structure in the daily rounds, the growing organs of the child will not get the start in life which they need. Foundations for good functioning of the organs are laid when there is a regular alternating between making that demand on the child and leaving her in peace. Many functional instabilities, in the sense of psychosomatic disorders in later life (automatic nervous system), have their roots in bad eating habits in early childhood. If children eat only according to fad and fancy, with no appetite at meal times because they have been constantly nibbling and snacking in-between, the digestive organs will fail to learn to work together strongly with regularity and then to relax. (Michaela Glöckler *Non-Verbal Education: A Necessity in the Developmental Stages*, in *Waldorf Journal Project #2*)

As a care provider for young children, as parent or teacher, we need to ask ourselves to what extent we foster the child's self education? It is important to create situations for the child where he can develop his own capacities and learn new skills by himself. Child's own activity, self initiated and achieved is so important. This develops the capacity for accepting - accepting self and accepting others. The lack of opportunity for this weakens the sense of self, self confidence and self-esteem. It is the adult's task to create an environment supportive of healthy development with ample opportunity for the child's own exploration and skill acquisition. Thereby we need to think deeply and broadly about what we want in this environment. In a kindergarten or home setting, the adult does have control over the creation of the surroundings, the choice of objects present, types of materials available, colors of paint on the walls, temperature of the room, food available at mealtimes, everything needs to be thought about. One element of the work of the adult is to be attentive to the details. Consideration of all the details allows the child to thrive in a sea of healthy surroundings. What images are on the walls? How many? What does the adult choose to wear? 'Loud' patterns and prints and images can distract the children from their dream-like engagement with the surroundings. What about jewelry on the adult's arms and hands? Does the adult wear her hair in the same style every day to not wake the child up by his noticing what is different? Perfumes need to be avoided both because of how overpowering and distracting they can be, and because the olfactory sense located in the nose has the shortest and most direct pathway of the senses in the brain. The carrier chemicals in perfumes definitely need to stay out of the children's noses.

What are the sense impressions being received by the child? These are the building blocks for their body and soul and need adult attention to ensure they are supportive to the child's development. Is the environment over stimulating with too many sense impressions, the walls too busy with decorations and posters and art, and too many toys (it is even possible to have too many 'Waldorf' style toys). Sensory overload give the children sensory indigestion, the quantity of images received by the child is literally indigestible for them. Each individual child has their own personal threshold for this, but as a theme, less is more in this realm.The young child has a tremendous power for transforming objects and situations into something other based on fantasy or imagination. It is important to support this transformative activity of play by providing items for their play that are full of possibility. Maybe instead of a play kitchen with bowls, have a wooden crate and some large shells. Those items could be a stove and bowls, or they could be so many other things. The imagination is the limit. Toys can be whatever is available. The more transforming the child needs to do in play the better. If the children have to fill in from their own imagination what is needed to make a toy or play object 'real,' then this work of imagination is enhancing the forming of the child's brain, the neural pathways

So many kindergartens and homes are over-filled with toys which then leaves the child little room for creating out of his own imagination and lots of busy-ness for the senses.

We are working with the reality of educating the will of the young child. It is will education to make a toy while the child is watching. Will education is making a wooden crate for kindergarten while the children are watching, and perhaps some are even helping. The child learns that first of all, it can be done. Human beings can make things, and the children can even make things. We are continuing the work of the creator beings in ways that are easily experienced. "Oh, we make stuff if we need it".

And the adult taking raw materials and making something from them is an example for the child's imagination. This type of activity stimulates the child's imagination into creative mobility. The imagination resonates with the activity of making when encountering it. This resonance works deeply into the child's soul and into their physical body. It stimulates the formative forces working in the brain and works deeply into the developing breathing and circulatory systems. The activities of making nourish and energize the young child's will forces. When an adult makes a toy in front of the child, a doll or wooden animal for example, the child's will is stimulated by the creating power of the will of the adult. Making is will activity, and is a dwindling art. We all can be makers! Through making we immerse the young child in our engaged will.

Creating an environment in which the child is allowed to imitate what he experiences, and explore what he can touch, hold, taste and climb on and under, without restriction is a worthy consideration. It is so common for the words "Stop" and "Don't" to be the ones most often heard by the young child. The child needs to explore and move freely. The kindergarten and the child's home need to be set up so that the children aren't continually hearing from the adults what they can't do. The child's impulse towards activity needs to be supported, not squashed.

Part of the thinking in creating an environment for young children is how the environment can foster creativity and imagination. First is to allow plenty of time for free play without intervention and interruption. The actively observing adult is present with eyes open and mouth shut. We have to provide suitable toys – simple toys that allow the child to 'complete' them with his own imagination. The brain develops when it does the work for which it was given. Exercise the brain with imagination. We have to provide the children with contact with the elements and the world of nature, making sure the children have enough 'outside time' to play in and explore. And we must provide examples of real work – the true engaged will of the adult.

Is there time for the child to engage in artistic activities supplies available that allow the child to freely express what is within them out of their own initiative? Nourishing images in stories and circle time need to be offered as seed imaginations to be taken up in play, as well as for numerous other reasons. Margret Meyerkort once said, "There could be a sign above the entrance to kindergarten that would say, 'There is always time in kindergarten.'" Life serves the young child to the fullest when their world feels relaxed and not rushed; they feel that there is enough time. And when the activity must end for whatever reasons, the adult gives enough time for ending the activity as well.

I have visited numerous early childhood programs, and have had many adult visitors to my kindergarten, and many of these teachers have had a similar habit of nearly constant singing or humming while the children are present. This is part of the environment we are creating, the aural realm. For me this is another kind of background noise, similar to having the radio or TV constantly on. The children need (yes, NEED) plenty of quiet, still time where they are initiating the sounding, where the environment if free from distracting noise, even if it is melodically beautiful and in the mood of the fifth. The quiet, yet attentive and fully present adult is they key to supporting the young child's experience.

Silence is golden! Yet silence is not something highly valued by the culture we live in. Just listen to the sounds of modern life all around us. We resist the experience of quiet; perhaps we even are afraid of silence. As child-carers we can model for the children and parents alike being comfortable with silence, actually enjoying silence. Meditative practice requires sitting still with silence. If we want children to grow up with the capacity for their own meditative life, we have to show them that we both value and practice silence.

What on earth is wrong with modern people that makes us bent on doing whatever we can to chase away the silence? Are we afraid of it? . . .Silence may be scary, but a lack of silence is much scarier. Those who don't seek occasional silence to make contact with their deeper core, higher self, pure soul, Buddha nature or whatever you want to call it, become detached from God. As a yogi friend said, 'To hear the voice of God, you must be silent.' I asked why. He looked at me as if the answer were obvious. 'Because God whispers.' (Tijn Touber, *Because God Whispers* in *Ode Magazine*, July/August 2008)

We can allow the children to be in the quietude of their inner life as they experience the outer world, or to initiate the talking to which we respond. We don't need to intrude into their world - why chat for the sake of chatting to fill a void? Can we become agents of renewing the practice and valuing of silence and simply being present?

A wonderful new resource about the importance and practice of silence is Robert Sardello's book *Silence; The Mystery of Wholeness*. (Goldenstone Press, 2008).

The adult must be sparing with their attention and with their *I* contact with young children, as it can easily overpower the young child. The adult has a strongly developed sense of self, and the young child does not. For some children, eye to eye contact is intimidating.

Six year old Josh was singing along in Circle Time. He was fully engaged in participating, and was loud and off key. I was a first year kindergarten teacher, and I looked at him to see what he was up to. I saw he was just loud and off-key, but giving his all. I was looking at him and he happened to notice I was looking at him. He immediately stopped singing altogether, and had a sort of a sheepish look on his face. I had broken his engagement with my I contact, and he became self-conscious and embarrassed.

Play is the critical tool for vast areas of development in the young child. As adults, we have to make the time and space available for sufficient, creative and explorative play. Through play the children come to grasp the world of social interaction, as well as their physical surroundings. It is both natural and social science for the young child, in a directly experiential way.

One aspect of the environment created by the adult for the young child is the materials available for play, and this deserves plenty of attention. What sorts of objects do we want to provide, and made of what materials? The example of the adult engaged in real work is so supportive of development and provides behaviors to be imitated in the play. One role of the adult is to welcome the child into the community of human working by doing work as example and with the young children. The adult's work is the tasks that need attention; the children's work is their play.

Often the child wants the adult to play with them, and this is a great way of connecting with the young child. We need to consider how much of their play time we want to engage with them in this way. A child can develop a habit of being entertained by the adult, and it then becomes hard for them to be self-sufficient in their play. And sometimes the adult has work that needs attention, like making a meal or folding laundry.
In kindergarten, one day I was ironing and folding the napkins and placemats. "Steve, will you be a dog with us?" "I'll be a dog, but I'll be a dog right here doing the ironing." "Okay."
An adult can't actually play like a child. The true play of the young child calls for total engagement in the imaginative

transformation of the world, adults can only pretend. The adult can be present, near the child's play, and engaged in adult activities. This example of working can be a stimulus for the child's play. The adult may of course initiate play, but needs to be aware of his or her role and the effect on the children, and know when to leave the children to play on their own terms. Children should not depend on adults to participate in their games nor on adult attitudes. Free play will come from the children's own imagination, inspired by adults' working, songs, and stories, as well as everyday events.

If the adults are engaged in calm, purposeful activity, the children are likely to imitate in their play, or even want to participate in the activity. Mending, sewing, washing, sweeping, repairing toys, etc. are among the activities for the teacher to be involved in while the children explore the room, play, draw, and so on. When conversation is kept to a minimum -- both with adults and with the children - the children can be more deeply engaged with their play. The atmosphere created by adults engaged in such purposeful activity, creates a protective and nurturing environment for the child in which he can either help with the chores, or explore the world through play.

Physical and social boundaries are also important on the path of a healthy developing sense of self. The self can only find itself when it meets boundaries. It is a boundary when the child has a drive to stand yet cannot yet. It experiences the probable frustration of being unable, and what it feels like to push through, to keep trying, and develop a new skill or capacity. This is one type of boundary experience. When he runs toward the curb with no sign of slowing before leaping into the street, and the parent loudly says, "Stop!" That is a boundary. He experiences the concern and love coming from the parent, and his trust in his parent grows, even if his words are complaining. It is the same with social boundaries.

Carmen was a five-year-old girl in my kindergarten. She was very fiery, very verbal, and very strong about getting her own way. One day she went over to a group of children and knocked over the house they were building. "We leave each other in peace," said Steve. And we helped them rebuild. A short time later she did it again, and a short time later again, and this time hit one of the other children. I picked her up and sat down with her on my lap. "Hands are for work and for taking care of others," I said as I held her hands gently. She squirmed to get up, saying she was going to do it again. I held her firmly. She squirmed and squirmed, and then she said to me, "I am gonna call my mom and she is gonna call the police and they are gonna come and take you away." I did not respond, but held her gently yet firmly. After two or three minutes she deeply exhaled and I could feel she was settled. I let her go with no more words. She played cooperatively for a few minutes and then came to me and said, "Steve, I love you," and then resumed her play. She was peaceful and cooperative for the remainder of the day.

She found a social boundary, kicked and screamed at it, and then relaxed in the security of it. She found herself there, at the boundary, and she found and recognized the loving guidance of her kindergarten teacher.

The way to develop sustainable living habits is by practicing them yourself at home and in kindergarten. If we think that cleaning up after a meal is a worthy activity with social and hygienic value, then we do the cleaning with the children present and participating. Some can wash and dry dishes, some sweep the floor, wipe the tables, take the compost to the compost pile, and so on. It is essential life activity - pedagogical activity! If we want the children to recycle, then we must both recycle ourselves, and make it practical and convenient for the children to participate. Where is the recycling bin in kindergarten or at home, is it east to get to? If we buy grains at the store in a bag, plastic or otherwise, can we be sure to clean and fold the bag, ready to use it another day; and then bring that bag to the store the next time. Even better - have a number of cloth bags stored and ready to carry our food and other supplies. The children see these items coming to kindergarten in reusable bags. This winter, we made and decorated cloth bags for the parents as a holiday gift from the children. If one of our wooden chairs breaks, we fix it. We mend and repair what needs repair, from chairs to dolls to children's pants and aprons. Whatever needs fixing, I always attempt to fix it myself before I call in a 'paid expert.' Perhaps if I don't have the tools or skills, I ask a parent to help, and have them do it when the children are present.

Habits of re-using, repairing, recycling, are learnable through imitation. The attitude of respect for what we have and its source can be passed on to the children through example. We fix what we have, we don't have to throw it away and get a new one. It is based on the adult's inner attitude of respect for the gifts of nature and the world, an attitude of gratitude. If we want to develop a 'green' culture of sustainability and ecological conservation, it starts with us and our actions and attitudes around the young children. They will grow into adults with ecological consciousness.

In my kindergarten, when something breaks, usually the children first try to fix it themselves. There always are one or two repair specialists that actually have the skills for many types of repairs. If those children can't do the repair, they bring it to me. We have created a culture of fixing and mending. One aspect of that is to acknowledge the situation right away, "We will mend this," even if it will be awhile, or even another day, before repairs can begin. I always make sure to get to the repair project when the children are present, and not let it slide and end up forgotten.

Steiner said how it is important to bring life activities into the kindergarten, to surround the young children with real life. These life activities, life giving and life sustaining activities such as cooking, cleaning, gardening, 'housework,' etc… are nurturing the developing etheric body, the life body, of the child which will not, in a sense, be born until age 6 or 7. Life activities support the development of the life senses, the foundation for truly social life.

The whole point of a preschool or kindergarten is to give young children the opportunity to imitate life in a simple and wholesome way. This task of adjusting life as one carries it out in the presence of the child in a meaningful, purposeful way, according to the needs of each child, is in accordance with the child's natural and inborn need for activity and is an enormously significant educational task. (R. Steiner, 4/18/24)

What are real life activities – they are real AND they are life based, need-based activities. At home or in the kindergarten, there are always domestic chores to be done - washing place mats and napkins; hanging them to dry; ironing, preparing and cooking meals, cleaning up after meals, weeding, pruning, raking leaves, and on and on. Both indoors and outdoors, there is plenty of work necessary for the maintenance of home and garden life. When we engage our adult will forces on this meaningful work, both the developing will and the developing etheric body of the children are strengthened. The children benefit from being surrounded by loving adults engaged in meaningful work such as housekeeping activities. The taking up of household tasks gives the children a sense of calm purpose and meaningful work. These activities help to create a sheath warmth and protection around the children in our presence. And when the adult is meaningfully and joyfully engaged in their work, the children play more peacefully, creatively and cooperatively. It is the magic example of the adult's engaged will for the child.

Adults engaged in the domestic arts (cooking, cleaning, building, etc…) provide real work examples that stream into the play of children and are very much in need because of the children's widespread lack of experiences of housework done in the home.

Kindergarten has to take on some aspects of what the home once stood for; the home is no longer the heart center of the family, but has become a resting place in between errands, activities and appointments, to which parents and children are often on their way. Waldorf early childhood centers more and more have become a replacement for certain aspects of the traditional home. They are a place where there is enough time and where housework is lovingly taken up and accomplished with participation from children. Providing a home-like environment for children gives them the opportunity to do things out of their own initiative. And the children need time, enough time. We need to create the feeling of 'There is no rush. There is time to play.'

Domestic activities, housework, taking care of the surroundings; all of these take us out of the personal and into the social realm. Caring for one's surroundings is a social gesture. We work together and for each other! The basis of our community life is the home, and social responsibility starts there.

Linda Thomas, whose cleaning company cares for the Goetheanum in Dornach, Switzerland says:.

There exists a great difference between cleaning and caring. When we clean, we remove dirt, and the result of cleaning sometimes does not even last five minutes. At the Goetheanum, you have barely cleaned the hallway, and already someone walks over it, leaving footprints everywhere. The same goes for parents with young children. For this very reason, many people consider cleaning a frustrating and unrewarding activity, a troublesome necessity.

Yet, we should try to do this task with our full awareness, with all our love. Once we learn to consciously penetrate each little corner with our fingertips, then cleaning takes on a nurturing aspect and becomes caring. What is so wonderful about it is that the result of caring lasts consider- ably longer than the result of removing dirt! When we have taken special care of a room, the little bit of fresh dirt that is brought in is barely disturbing—one can live with it. The glow is totally different from areas where layers of dirt and grime have built up. Lately, a new cleaning culture, which we should really try to prevent, is trying to establish itself. There is supposedly a spray for everything—you spray and you wipe away—not much water is needed! One does indeed remove a small quantity of dirt, but instead of caring for a surface, you leave a chemical layer behind, containing quantities of dissolved dirt.

*While caring for a room, we do not only come into contact with the physical world. The whole atmosphere changes, the room is filled with light. Especially children react strongly to this transformation, and they also seem to perceive the change directly. (*Linda Thomas, *Chaos in Everyday Life: About Cleaning and Caring, from Gateways,* Issue 45, Fall/*Winter* 2003*)*

How can we redeem housework, the thinking of housework as drudgery, so we provide a positive example for the children.? We can find joy in the work and express it in our movement and our gestures. We can bring order and planning to our work and finish it. Some projects take more than one time to complete, but persistence over time is important for the child to observe. All of these, though, are self-discipline on the part of the adult, and hard work at first.

We can cultivate an attitude of looking for work that needs doing. That is a real gift to the children. Rather than, "What should I do with the children today?" we can say, "What needs to be done, and how do I do it?"

Taking care of our body and our surroundings are most important. For me, crafts projects are not as high a priority, though a craft project as a part of the preparation for a festival becomes a meaningful element in the life of home or kindergarten. For example, the making of a card for a birthday, or gifts for Mothers Day. But a project "to give the children something to do" is superficial. Crafts and projects with the children can be support of creativity and motor skill development, but they don't exercise the will unless they come for the child's initiative. If the adult has a sewing project that needs doing, perhaps a cloth has torn, of course have extra materials available as the children will also want to sew. And you can help them along as needed. Five- and six-year-olds will sometimes want to make something to bring into their imaginative play – perhaps a doll or puppet. But then it comes out of the child engaging herself, out of her own initiative, and based on imitation – the will is exercised and strengthened.

Domestic activities anchor the child in the world – both the physical world, and the social world in which we live. Our housework provides a healthy example for imitation. We are helping to make the children truly capable, and helping them toward their future with strong will forces.

It happens from time to time that a child is out of sorts and they are not able to play constructively, either by themselves, or in the social setting. A magical cure for that child is helping out with some real work that needs doing. Folding the laundry or cutting the vegetables is an opportunity for the child to get grounded into the work, and the obstacle to relaxed and peaceful play they may have been experiencing dissolves. A few minutes later one hears, "I want to go play now." The adult can feel that the child is really ready to play. Their fantasy or imagination has woken up again from a small dosage of meaningful work.

Janet Kellman once spoke about the myth of quality time. What is "quality time?" Many adults think 'special' time going to 'special' places is more valuable than other activities; it has more connecting going on. Quality time really is measured by how truly present one is with the children, while one is supporting their developmental needs, the needs of the developing soul, etheric body, and will of the young child. Connect with the children while immersing them in life activities, activities that nurture and sustain life.

Connected to this is the importance of creating healthy rhythms in the child's life. Rhythm is the lifeblood of the ether body, so we need to establish regular eating times and not-eating times, rest and sleep and waking times, hygiene times and so on. Steiner spoke about how important it is to teach the children to breathe, and a healthy rhythm is a breathing in itself, and a teaching for the child's life body to create its own rhythm form.

...the breathing is the most important mediator between the outer physical world and the human being who is entering it. But we must also be aware that this breathing cannot yet, by any means, function so as fully to maintain the life of the body...To express it roughly we may say: the child cannot yet breathe in the right inner way, and education will have to consist in teaching the child to breathe rightly. (R. Steiner, *Study of Man,* p. 20-21)

Through the child's experience of a rhythmic life, habits of hygiene can be developed – these good habits can be formed gently. Additionally, when the daily habit rhythm includes coming indoors and changing into 'indoor shoes,' when just before eating hands are washed, then there is no conflict around these activities. Rhythm of daily life is like the tide, the tide comes and goes whether or not you participate or desire it. "I don't want to wash my hands," just doesn't arise. In the life of adults with young children, rhythm replaces conflict, and gives the strength of flow the carries along adults and children alike.

To help the child become more receptive to fellow human beings, a climate of helping each other needs to be developed, a culture of service. *The most important thing is to establish an education through which human beings learn once more how to live with one another.* (Rudolf Steiner, *The Younger Generation,* October 1922 p. 149/150)

What can we do to help and support each other? Sally says, "I didn't play with these toys. I just colored today." Teacher replies, "In kindergarten we all help, we all tidy up." We set the table for each other. Some children help prepare lunch, but it is for all to eat. One child can be the server of the food, and they have to wait until they have served all the others before they sit down to eat. In my kindergarten, when it is someone's birthday, they have the privilege of serving the cake their parents and kindergarten mates. If someone falls and scrapes her knee, the basket of bandaids and healing salve can be gotten by another child. My kindergarten is for children three-years old until they go on to first grade. In a mixed-age group setting it is easy to foster empathy and service and social responsibility. "Jill, your inside shoes are already tied. Please tie Jackson's so we can all go in." It is socially important to have a mixed-age span. The younger children learn to play by observing older children at play. And older children learn to be gentle and nurturing when younger children are part of the group. The older children also develop skills of caring for and helping the younger ones. Everyone learns to adjust to the give-and-take of the social life in the mixed age kindergarten. Each one learns that personal needs will be met, but sometimes we have to wait. "Everyone's needs will be met but not necessarily all at the same time" is a guiding motto. The children experience a kindergarten family that mirrors real community family life in which we have the opportunity to draw out of the children flexibility, tolerance, and generosity toward one another and individual needs.

It is socially important to have a mixed-age span. The younger children learn to play by observing older children at play. And older children learn to be gentle and nurturing when younger children are part of the group. The older children also develop skills of caring for and helping the younger ones. Everyone learns to adjust to the give-and-take of the social life in the mixed age kindergarten. Each one learns that personal needs will be met, but sometimes we have to wait. "Everyone's needs will be met but not necessarily all at the same time" is a guiding motto. The children experience a kindergarten family that mirrors real community family life in which we have the opportunity to draw out of the children flexibility, tolerance, and generosity toward one another and individual needs.

Another realm where one has an opportunity to bring social faculties to the children is the story. Here the images speak so powerfully and there is no need for explicit moralizing. In fact, the child must 'get' the truth of the story themselves or it will not penetrate into their inner life. The pictures, the images that are evoked by the telling of a story speak deeply into the child's heart. Story is a powerful potential factor in the child's own developing world view and brings them both knowledge of people and of the world as well as guidance in challenging situations. The stories one tells need to resonate inwardly as describing truths. I tell stories of redemption, stories of courage, wisdom and kindness overcoming evils. I tell stories of patience, persistence and compassion. These themes are present in the folk and fairy tales from all over the world. Some special stories for me include, from South Africa, 'The Winning of Kwelanga,' and "Nkosnati and the Dragon," Grimm's 'The Queen Bee' and from the Chippewa people 'Shingebiss.' Story speaks so powerfully even to adults. One has far more possibility of reaching into another's heart through story than through intellectual instructing and persuading.

Pleasure and delight are the forces that most properly enliven and call forth the organs' physical forms.........The joy of children in and with their environment, must therefore be counted among the forces that build and shape the physical organs. They need teachers that look and act with happiness and, most of all, with honest, unaffected love. Such a love that streams, as it were, with warmth through the physical environment of the children may be said to literally "hatch" the forms of the physical organs. (Rudolf Steiner, *The Education of the Child in the Light of Anthroposophy,* pps. 21/22)

Warmth is required for all development. If you have some leftovers from dinner, they go into the refrigerator, a cold place, so bacteria won't grow. If you want children to develop they need an atmosphere of warmth, both physical warmth and soul warmth. Children need the warmth of human interest and attention. For the young child to stay open to connecting, there must be a fabric of trust and intimacy, and this starts with true interest in the adult toward the child. To create the possibility for children connecting with the world and the cosmos, the adult must ensoul, enliven, enhance, enrich, engage, enthuse…..the adult must be active in his participation in the world, and active in connecting with the child. This is founded on the adult being a person connected to her inner joy, smiling and open to experiencing people and the world. An adult active in this way shines joy into all the details of her life and activities.

This verse from Rudolf Steiner is for the adult to contemplate in relation to the child or children in his care:

May light stream into you that can take hold of you
I follow its rays with the warmth of my love.
I think with my thinking's best thoughts of joy
On the stirrings of your hear
May they strengthen you
May they carry you,
May they cleanse you.
I want to gather my thoughts of joy
Before the steps of your life,
That they unite with your will for life
So that it finds itself with strength
In the world,
Ever more
Through itself.

Chapter 5

Language and Communicating

If any of this sounds like a rough translation
Please know, there are no words for these things
In any language.
This is a translation as sure as you're born,
Translated from unspeakable silence
Into English,
English as a second language.
Our first language must be silence.
All our best work is done in silence.
And our best work may not survive translation.
Jessica Ruby Simpson

A typically human form of relating is through the dynamic of speaking and listening, an interactive connecting through spoken language. It is a lifelong path to become more and more self aware in our own speaking. For parents and teachers of young children, it is especially important to be as conscious as possible in our speech and language with the children because they are developing their verbal communication habits and skills from our example. Particularly with children through kindergarten age, the content, tone and character of our speech even affects their physical and intellectual development.

As parents and teachers we can support the healthy development of the young child through our own speech. The clearer we speak, the better we enunciate, then the more the child will learn to speak more clearly - through imitation. Thoughtfully choosing our words creates a positive example for the child's own language. The child needs the example of what we really are: adults. The children learn their vocabulary, grammar and syntax from the example of the people speaking around them; learning language is through imitation and the parents and teachers are the main source of example. Clear speech is a foundation for clear thinking.

When I was a child, four times a year on TV was a seasonal special with Charlie Brown and Snoopy and the gang. The content of those shows is forgotten, but what I recall is the sound of the adults speaking. Whenever an adult spoke it was the sound of a trombone, "waah, waah, waah." Charlie Brown and his friends never got the content of the grow-ups' words, the tone of their voices conveyed sufficient message.

In the whole realm of speech and language in general, I think that adults talk too much and too long, especially when interacting with young children. Sometimes it seems like adult speaking is just to fill the space, so the silence is not allowed to be. Our modern world doesn't support silence and stillness, and maybe it has becomes most people's habit to avoid quiet moments. Music is constantly playing in stores, cafes, in our own cars – there is a sort of constant sonic companion so we don't have to be alone with ourselves. The young child <u>needs</u> quiet so he can be alone with his experiences and his thoughts and begin to process, digest and synthesize them. Children need experiences of being together with adults without the adult speaking. What adults can just wait, patiently present, for the child to initiate conversation? Few and far between!

Do we give the child room to initiate conversation, to use their own will in thinking? This requires adults to retrain ourselves to be able to live in the *silence*, and to allow the children to un-make the silence themselves? Can we as adults even learn to be comfortable being together with adults in silence?

"Never pass up an opportunity to be silent;" sage words spoken by one of Garrison Keillor's cowboy characters on his radio show *Prairie Home Companion.*

Real Life

A child is engaged peacefully in playing with wooden blocks. He has been at it for several minutes. The adult says, "Hey, did you know next week Grandma is coming over." The play with blocks is now over, and the child is dis-engaged.

The adult and child are walking together on a path in the woods. The child stops and bends down to see more closely a particular leaf. The adult says. "Look over there. That is a blue jay." Child looks to blue jay, leaving behind the experiencing the wonder of the leaf.

We adults have a tendency to think that our agenda, the things important to us, would also be of equal value to the child. Why do we think that? How is a blue jay more important than a leaf? It seems hard for adults to allow children the space to simply be; to allow the child to simply and deeply experience their own experiences of where the child's attention has been placed.

Teachers and parents must learn to hold back their own desires and expectations for the child and understand how important it is for the child to learn how to meet life's experiences and challenges on his own and in his own time. Most children of today are over-supervised and over-protected. They barely have the chance to feel their own feelings without having someone probe and push them toward abstract thinking.

Becoming an active observer is a worthy goal for early childhood educators and the parents of the young child. This is a worthy practice that one can develop into a capacity - a capacity that supports the development of any young children in your personal world. Yet rather than actively observing and practicing holding back, often the adult takes over and is very much 'in the child's business.'

I would like to know why it is that we have disregarded all children's significantly spontaneous and comprehensive curiosity... Nothing seems to be more prominent about human life than its wanting to understand all and put everything together. (R. Buckminster Fuller)

Harvard psychologist and author Burton White researched what factors determine that a child is intelligent and happy. He searched for a common demographic or psychological characteristics that distinguished which children would be the one child in 30 that becomes an adult who is brilliant and happy. His sampling of children came from a wide diversity of backgrounds including geographically, economically, family size, single parents and two-parent homes, and level of parents' education. The only common factor he discovered is that the bright and happy adults all spent considerable time 'spacing out,' simply staring quietly, their thoughts kept to themselves, when they were children.

You are troubled at seeing him spend his early years in doing nothing. What! Is it nothing to be happy? Is it nothing to skip, play, and run around all day long? Never in his life will he be so busy as now. (Jean-Jacques Rousseau, *Émile: Or, Concerning Education*)

How often have you observed an adult holding a crying young child when the adult breathes in sharply, "Huhhh! Look!" The child is feeling sad; he is feeling his own feeling of sadness. The adult has an agenda of distracting him from his sadness. *Is distracting the child from his feelings helpful in the moment?* Maybe he stops crying. *Is it helpful in the long run?* No, the child hasn't had the opportunity to be with his own feelings. Additionally, Steiner advised that we must teach the children how to breathe. (*Study of Man*, lecture 1, Aug. 21, 1919) This is an example of teaching them (by imitation) how not to breathe.

When a child is crying from a physical or emotional hurt I like to simply be with him at first, just present, perhaps holding him on my lap, not asking him what happened. Just sitting together. I do not tell him to 'stop crying.' After a bit of time, he usually tells me what hurt what he thinks caused it. Sometimes after a bit of just being with him, I verbally check-in, "I see you are sad. Does your body hurt somewhere?" And see where it leads.

One can be with someone, totally connecting, without speaking. Merely through each other's presence, through simple, attentive presence, no words are necessary, there is a soul/spiritual exchange taking place. This exchange is refreshing and renewing in ways spoken conversation often is not.

When adults do speak to children, it is sensible to be aware of the speed of our speaking. Adults tend to talk fast, especially when the subject seems important to the adult. Yet actively slowing down our speaking can often be all it takes for our message to get through.

Wichita State University audiology professor Ray Hull has researched the rate of adults' speech in relation to the processing capacity of the maturing central nervous system in young children. He found that adults who speak too rapidly can overload children's central nervous systems and, in turn, inhibit their ability to learn. Hull's research shows that the average adult speaks between 160 and 170 words per minute (wpm) while the average child age 5 to 7 can process speech at a maximum rate of 124 wpm. When teachers and parents speak more quickly than young children can understand, the intended message cannot get across, and intended learning can be hindered. In the young child, what may sometimes appear as inattention is simply not being able to process at the speed with which the words were spoken. The child will simply not be able to understand as well or retain the information.

If you slow down your rate of speech from 170 wpm to 124 wpm, the speech sounds become more distinct, the vowels and consonants sound more clearly for the listening young child. When we begin to articulate speech more slowly we are increasing the understandability of what is being said. (Dinkel, Dana, *WSU professor researches how to speak to children,* Wichita State Univ.)

One child, on the first day of kindergarten said to me, "Steve, you talk slow." At our first parent conference some weeks later, the parent asked, "How come he listens to you."

Singing to the children can sometimes be an effective tool in getting the child's attention or even getting him to do what you want, especially if used sparingly. It is certainly a gentle way to get someone's attention, especially when they are otherwise engaged. When young children are fully engaged in some activity or work/play, and you want their attention, a singing voice delivering the message you are wanting can often get through when speaking might just not be noticed.

Intervention

Adults intervene so often in the affairs of children, in their play exploration, and their social interactions - in general, too often. A new term has entered our culture to describe this; "helicopter parent." You have seen them. They are always hovering close to the children and engaging in pre-emptive intervening without giving the children a chance to learn how to work it out for themselves. Surely it is important to ensure that the children are safe on both physical and soul levels, but if we as adults are always intervening then the children don't have the space necessary to learn for themselves. I always ask myself, 'Is this a situation where I need to intervene?' and 'Do I need to intervene yet?' Learning for the young child requires trying things out for themselves, so how can we balance giving plenty of room for self initiated learning, exploration without intervention, with soul and physical safety considerations. From my perspective, I see adults intervening too much and too soon so much of the time. Becoming the active observer is far better than taking over the child's world.

Some Basics

Central to my assessment of any situation with young children is an awareness of the different developmental stages of consciousness in children. *What is the consciousness to whom I am speaking?* Then can I determine if and how to respond.
If one chooses to speak, keep in mind that it is more important how something is said than the words used, the verbal content. An underlying stream of intent flows from the speaker to the child's soul through the tone, the modulation of voice pitch or

accentuation of the sounds. Because of the child's strongly developed sense of hearing, but not so fully developed sense of word, the character or quality of the speaking is of more consequence than the verbal content.

One basic guideline for me is to speak with clarity and brevity. Speak what you mean in a clear and concise manner. Be direct with as few words as possible. And speak your truth, speak from a place of honesty. It is important to say what you mean, and mean what you say. Remember Dr. Suess' Horton the Elephant? He had a kind of integrity important to model, "I said what I meant and I meant what I said; an elephant is faithful one hundred percent."

Consider these scenarios:

A mother is at the park with her four-year-old son. He runs from one climbing structure to the next. She rushes to catch up to him and says, "Thanks for waiting." Her meaning was that she was unhappy, even angry, that he did not wait for her, and her tone was sarcastic, but her words were of thanks. What message do you suppose gets through to the child?

The parents are out and Grandma is visiting with her grandchild. She notices he is drawing with crayons on the newly refinished hardwood floor. "What are you doing?" says Grandma.

Mom notices child with crayons drawing on newly refinished hardwood floor. "WHAT ARE YOU DOING?"

Both use the same words, but clearly grandma is actually wondering what the child is doing, while mom with her tone is telling the child he is doing something WRONG. Grandma was asking a question, mom was using the same question to make a statement about the wrongness of the child's action.

Didn't You Understand?

Another use of the English language that is troubling for me is using a negative when seeming to ask a question- "Don't you think…", "Didn't you…." "Didn't you already put the toys away?" "Didn't you hear what I said?" It smacks of shaming because the speaker means, "Why aren't the toys put away yet, you were supposed to do that?" "I can see since you didn't do what I told you to, you didn't listen to what I said." It is a confusing use of language when used with adults, and with young children it serves to create a schism in the experience between the words used and the intention of the speaker. And of course, the imitating young child takes up this practice of 'shame speaking.'

I visited an early childhood program. Seated with the children at the table, I observed the following. The table was set for lunch. The children were chatting merrily away, and the teacher and assistant approached the table with the food in bowls. The children continued to chat. The teacher stood quietly a moment and said, "I'm waiting." And she waited.
The children continued to chat. Soon the assistant said, "Teacher is waiting." And they both waited, standing beside the table. Finally the assistant raised her voice and said, "Teacher is waiting to serve the food until you are quiet." The children quieted down, and lunch began.

I wondered what the point was of announcing the teacher was waiting. Yes, she was waiting. That was obvious. Perhaps the situation could have unfolded more smoothly if the teacher said what she probably really meant, something like, "Before I serve the food, I want quiet at our table. "

Yes Means Yes and No Means Yes

One of the children in my kindergarten gave with profound clarity a powerful picture of a major challenge the children face.

He perhaps was speaking about his parents, or about many parents, when he said, "Yes means yes and no means yes."

Children quickly learn when one does not say what they mean. Often children discover that when a parent or teacher says, "No," it means "Keep asking and I'll say yes." This is the foundation of why children learn to whine to get what they want.

Today there is a large degree of uncertainty living in adults, we are aware that we don't really understand a lot of what is going on in the world. We have lost confidence in our own thinking and decision making. Some adults seem unable to form opinions or make decisions. In early childhood children experience many levels of everything that confronts them. They look to the adult for the meaning of their experiences and feel secure in that. They are looking to the adult for confidence and clarity of judgment. Without this decisiveness in the adults, the children lose their own confidence, and develop anxiety due to a feeling of insecurity.

In the same vein, one sees young children offered so many choices today, beyond what they are capable of making sound decisions about. The young child is not able to understand in the same way as an adult, their neurology is not mature and their reasoning ability is not available yet. The child expects guidance from adults, without this guidance, the child is insecure and confused. Insecurity is weakening for the formation of his mind and body. Too much choice leads to insecurity and, ironically, a lack of self reliance.

There is a cultural movement to *adultify* the child as soon as possible. Parents are taught to empower the young child to be the decider. Young children need the security and certainty of adult guidance. They are not yet ready for major decisions. There is enough stress already in children's lives in the modern world. A certain amount of choice is healthy and important; to empower a young child to be as equal with adults in negotiating decisions is not. That would be the empowering of an irrational being. We adults must assume responsibility for guiding young children.

All parents want their children to grow up to become free human beings, but the misconception is strong that one must therefore allow their young child to be free, to be the chooser and to not to follow directions. So the three-year-old is asked what he wants to eat or what clothes he would like to wear. The grown-up has a lack of confident clarity about what is right and fears a conflict with the child so leaves the choice to him.

"It's cold out, do you want to wear your coat? "No, mommy."

"What do you want for breakfast today?" "I don't know." "Do you want pancakes? Or waffles?" "Nooo." "Eggs, or cereal?" "I don't know."

Some choice is essential, and as the child gets older, more and more choice is important. For a young child, small areas of choice are enough.
"We're having eggs and bread for breakfast today. Do you want your bread toasted?"

When someone gives their time and energy and thoughtfulness to preparing a meal, it is important that this is honored. When dinner is made, and the table laid, and the child doesn't want the food on the table, "Well, do you want a peanut butter sandwich instead?" What kinds of habits are we helping to develop in the child?

Children of this age learn through example and sense on s many levels. The thereby take in the uncertainty in the adult's attitude. True freedom can only develop in adulthood when one has been led though the early years of childhood with the example of the clear guidance of adults.

Please, Okay?

Often there is subtly offered choice as well, present in the very commonly used word 'okay.' It so frequently is used as a question in itself. A typical scenario: a mother of a kindergarten child ushers her child into the room. She stays a few minutes to see that her child is settled and then says, "I'm going now, OK.?" The child replies, "No," which frustrates the mother. How about, "I'm going now. I'll be back at pick-up time."

Or, a kindergarten teacher decides to intervene in the children's play. She says, "It's Tommy's turn now, okay?" Is that a question really? "I'm not sure if I mean it or not, so can Tommy have a turn?" How about, "It's Tommy's turn now. You may have a turn next." The children are far more secure when they feel a confident guidance from the adult that cannot come with checking with the child if your resolution of the situation works for them or not. "Okay?"

What creeps into spoken interactions between adults and children sometimes could be described as a process of trying to manifest the wishes of the parents through the use of negotiation. When the parent is hoping and wishing for the child to comply with what she say, she tags on okay at the end of the statement. And sometimes it is an inner attitude of 'I sure hope he does what I want. What will I do if he doesn't?' that speaks just a loudly to the child. The child receives the message, 'You are in charge. I relegate my authority and responsibility as parent and will have you be the leader.'

Similarly, the word "please" is sometimes used when there actually is no choice being offered. It is a sort of demand with a 'please' added on, for instance, a child has just poked one of the chickens with a stick. "Hand me the stick, please." Instead, how about, "This stick needs a rest," while holding your hand open and palm up toward the child? I think we don't need to say please

98

when we really are offering no choice. I do say "Thank you" when the child has put the stick in my hand.

It is important that the adult has consistency in follow through. When the adult says such-and-such will be happening later, integrity requires that it does occur. Lack of this follow through leads the child to another picture of words speaking untruth.In early childhood, adult gestures and actions speak more clearly than words; the adult's example rather than her instruction in the key. Is there a way to get your message across non-verbally? Can non-verbal action accompany verbal interchange?

For instance, five year old Susie runs into the room, slamming the door behind her. One could stay seated and say to Susie, while she is across the room, "Next time, walk when you come in and please close the door quietly behind you."
Or one could get up and walk across the room to the door, opening it and saying, "We close the door gently." Then, while heading back to the chair, "We walk inside." *Words are accompanying the action!*

Many people use verbal instruction as a way to correct the behaviors of the young child. A young child understands the meaning of an action intuitively and then imitates the action, he or she is not at the stage of development to understand explanations about the deed. This is the sensory-motor stage of life when sense experience is the stimulation for action, not thinking before action. For the young child, meanings are not abstracted independently from the physical experience, but work directly through the sense perceptions into movement.
Experience and action operate as a unified, imitative process. In the most accurate way, children do what they see and speak what they hear. Everything that they experience is understood, in a sense, immediately in their body's depths, even if they have no words or concepts for it.

It is so important not to shorten the imitative phase by forcing a development of abstract thinking prematurely. Yet this is the result of the common practice of educating the young child by verbal instruction and explanation. This forced, early awakening of abstract intelligence also diminishes the capacity for imitation.

Although it is highly necessary in view of the nature of our modern civilization that a man should be fully awake in later life, the child must be allowed to remain as long as possible in the peaceful, dreamlike condition of pictorial imagination in which his early years are passed. For if we allow his organism to grow strong in this non-intellectual way, he will rightly develop in later life the intellectuality needed in the world today. (Rudolf Steiner, *Education and Modern Life*)

But

Another habit in common use in speaking is the widespread use of the word "but" – but it always is a subtle way to negate or deny something. For instance, "I know you want to get ice cream, but it is almost dinner time." Translated, the speaker is saying, "It doesn't matter what you think about ice cream, the important thing is that dinner is soon so no ice cream." In a sentence, 'but' undoes everything before the 'but.'

Praise?

Just recently, psychological research has confirmed that praise of the young child is not supportive of the development of self esteem; in fact it has the opposite effect. In a Columbia University study, they found that praise leads to goal oriented behavior and a difficulty in handling failure. Praise tends to be result-oriented, making the effort to achieve something devalued. Acknowledging the child's effort is far more valuable than praising the child's 'success,' and more valuable than praising certain characteristic like intelligence or niceness. We all want the children to develop self confidence and self esteem. Praising them is just not the way. Praise - the regular complimenting of the young child - awakens self-judgment. The young child naturally just *does;* he is active in his will in a non-self aware manner.

"That was good, Johnny" Johnny thinks, "Well, was it bad before when you didn't say anything? If you don't say, then is it not good?"
Jimmy thinks, "Well. If Johnny is good, then that must make me bad."

Susie is trying walking on a narrow board. She falls off, landing on her bottom. Teacher says, "Good job, Susie." Susie likely thinks something like, "Yeah right. I just fell off and failed in my attempt." What about just watching and Susie seeing you seeing her? Or, if you do comment, "That seems hard to do," or, "Good try, Susie." If some other children had been asking Susie to try for awhile, and she finally agreed, "I'm glad you tried that."

Praising in a general way is a catalyst for the waking up to one's self comparing his actions to others and it can create later self esteem issues. Different from praise is acknowledgement. Through acknowledging specific actions we transmit our values. Acknowledging tells you how what you did affects me? "I like that you brought the band-aids when Susie has a cut and needs one."

So what do we do when we bestow praise and reproof? "That's good," "right," or "well done," we say, and thereby hold a mirror before the child in connection with his particular activity. We thus destroy the empathic unity between the child and his engagement. We criticize - however positive our criticism may be. We take the child out of the activity in which he had been immersed, and we can graphically compare the child's experience to that of the fish taken out of the water, out of its

101

natural habitat. Steiner describes time and again how an independent body of life or body of formative forces takes on shape around the age of seven. Until then even praise is unwarranted, for our detached adult consciousness cuts into the unity of child and activity, into the merging consciousness, the will. We appeal to something which at this age the child does not have, and thus can cause uncertainty and frustration...
Take care not to rush into reproof. The young child does not distinguish between the action and the doer, so reproof is painful. He feels his very being, his essence, is blamed, is wrong, and he can withdraw into himself. (Margret Meyerkort and Rudi Lissau, *The Challenge of the Will*, pps. 47-48)

Ella finally threaded her needle after several minutes of trying. She had a big smile and looked to me to see if I had seen, if I had been interested in her attempt. I had seen and smiled back at her. We shared a knowing smile.

When the child, out of his own will, attempts and succeeds at a new activity, a big smile arises on his face. When you have been actively observing, a truly interested bystander, the child has exercised his will and leaned something new. And when you simply share a knowing smile it is far more valuable than any words of praise, or any words at all. You have shared a deep heart connecting, not a head experience.

Answering Children's Questions

Young children ask many questions! Sometimes it is that they have something to tell us. Answering with "Well...I wonder," or simply pausing a moment, allows him to tell us something, and gives him the space to offer his idea. Often a child will supply the answer to his own questions and reject the one given by the adult. The child has his own answer already, and just wants to tell us. Often the answers which young children give are more full of imagination and clarity than those which an adult offers.

A child asks: "Why is it raining?" And then adds, "Is it because the plants are thirsty?"
Or, "Why did you put the fence around the garden? It's to keep the chickens from digging there."

When we are called on to answer why and how and so on, we need to be creative and imaginative, and at the same time, honest and truthful in our responses. Long explanations with intellectual, scientific detail are not effective, and are even harmful to young children. "Why is it raining?" One answer, "It is the water cycle. There are the three processes of evaporation, condensation and precipitation. Rain is the precipitation stage." Or, as above, "The clouds are full of water and the plants are thirsty."

We need to nourish the imaginative dream consciousness of the young child, not reason them into intellectual wakefulness. We don't need to explain the differences between round and square, up and down, or teal and blue. They will learn to differentiate in their own time, out of their developmental readiness and their direct experiences of the world and through imitating the naming of things by adults.

It is not always easy for adults to take up an imaginative, succinct and direct way of answering questions. Our intellect gets in the way. Keep in mind the stage of the young child's consciousness. Offering intellectual explanations, regardless of how scientifically true, is like giving a thousand words when the picture will satisfy the child much more.

Can we develop the capacity to give answers that engage the child in activity, rather than closing them off with fixed concepts or abstract concepts? We are infected with the coldness and rigidity of intellectuality. The young child still lives in the warm movement of fantasy and imagination and creativity. Their later life of thinking depends on the movement of the body and the movement of imaginations; on rich, active imaginative language in early years. As adults, we need to learn to speak the truth in imaginative pictures. We need to learn to be poetic in our answers to the questions of the young children, not to give abstract and scientific responses. When children pass the age of six or seven, they do need much more explanation, more 'scientific' answers to their questions. Then they are anticipating an explanation in the answer, no longer so simply living into the speaking as does a young child.

For the young child, the world is still in a process of becoming, it is still being created. For the adult, the world already is, the world is being, not becoming. The world of the adult is being - stepping into the world of becoming is enlivening for the adult's thinking and etheric body, actually health enhancing.

When we as adults can give enlivened, imaginative responses to the questions of young children, our will is active in thinking in images, our imagination is powered by will.
When the will is active in thinking, we weave with warmth, the child experiences this warmth of engaged will forces. This warmth is the effect of the ego, the I, of the adult active in their willed thinking.

Questioning and Probing

Asked of the young child: "What did you do today?" "What story did Steve tell today?" "Who did you play with today?" "Oh, your shirt says Seattle. Have you been to Seattle? I went there once. What did you like about Seattle?"

Young children are asked so many questions. Questions call on one to think and remember. What is happening to the child who has been asked a question to which she can have no immediate answer, and who is "bearing down," gritting her mental teeth, trying to give an answer? "…Umm…" It is as if smoke begins to pour out of the ears as the premature thinking is trying to be active. If we really are observing, it is painful to see. "What happened in kindergarten today? Tell me everything you did." Rather, we can let the child talk about her experiences in her own time, out of the capacity of her own budding memory. It is healthier for the child if we do not drag and pull information out! Not remembering all the details of her day says the child has been allowed to live in her imaginative world. Traumatic experiences are the ones most likely to be talked about, as they are consciousness awakening. For most adults, in fact, the earliest memory that can be recalled is of an injury or emotional hurt.

Children's Feelings

In our modern world with trends toward child empowerment and "getting in touch with our feelings," we often hear this type of interaction between adult and young child: "How do you think you would feel…? Or "Do you know how he feels?" Young children are called on to "get in touch" with their feelings and the feelings of others. They are not yet ready to intellectualize, to bring to consciousness their feelings. They are also not yet ready for the abstract activity of figuring out what someone else might be feeling. The barely, if at all, are able to name their own feelings. Certainly they experience feelings, but they will come to label them when they are ready, in their own time. And we can help them to learn names for their feelings, for example, "Johnny is sad. He was not yet done playing with that toy." (Johnny will let you know if you read his feeling incorrectly, "No, I am mad.") We don't ask the child what he is feeling, we attempt to name it, as an educated guess. We acknowledge the child's feelings, but avoid probing and intellectualizing in the feeling realm until a later stage of mental and emotional development when the intellect and awareness of their own feelings have come into active duty.

I read an account of a woman in her late twenties describing her experience growing up. (Unfortunately the book title has eluded me.) Her parents constantly asked her how she was feeling about this and that and she describes being confused by their questions. She was regularly asked why she felt the certain feelings she was having; Why are you sad? What are you angry about? She explained how she developed a habit of questioning her own feelings rather than feeling them. This is what she was trained for by her parents in their consistent asking her about her feelings. As an adult, she always analyses her feelings, never allowing her feelings to just be. She lives her feeling life now, as an adult, in her head.

Reasoning, probing, and intellectualizing disconnect children from their doing, from their life of full engagement with their world. The child is awakened from a unity with her surroundings and activities into self-consciousness and a different kind of awareness of the world. All too often we see precocious children, children who have been "pushed" awake, who look pale and wan. They are drained of the precious etheric forces of growth, and this can only have adverse effects in later years.

NVC - Nonviolent Communication

There are some common habits in speech that if eliminated lead to more direct, honest and connecting communicating. All too often people add interpretation and judgments to what they observe. In our thinking we tend to blame others for our won feelings, and it is hard to let others know what is really important to us.

One day, my youngest daughter (about age five) had been playing with some toys and cooking utensils. I had a plan for us to go out to the beach, and didn't want to leave an un-tidy house. I told her, "You need to clean up your room." And suddenly I heard what I had said. I mean, I really heard it and understood what I was saying. It was a profound moment of self-discovery for me. Rosemary did not need to clean her room. If anything, it was my need, more accurately my desire, for a tidy house. It surely was not any need of hers. This was a revelation and it has led to my becoming more and more aware of my own thinking as it is revealed in what I say. At times my thinking about speaking has become nearly obsessive on my path of self awakening in communicating. I have found myself, especially with children, using less words, and words that more accurately reflect reality. I try to stay away form making demands (You need to…) and I speak from my truth.

At around the same time in my life as this event, I encountered the work of Marshall Rosenberg, author of *Nonviolent Communication; A Language of Life*. Rosenberg developed an approach to liberating ourselves from old habits of blame and demands in our thinking and communicating. Practicing such a path of spiritual development is a gift for the children (and all others) in our lives.

NVC [Nonviolent Communication] is founded on language and communication skills that strengthen our ability to remain human, even under trying conditions. It contains nothing new; all that has been integrated into NVC has been known for centuries. The intent is to remind us about what we already know – about how we humans were meant to relate to one another – and to assist us in living in a way that concretely manifests this knowledge…I developed NVC as a way to train my attention – to shine the light of consciousness – on places that have the potential to yield what I am seeking. What I want in my life is compassion, a flow between myself and others based on a mutual giving from the heart…NVC helps us connect with each other and ourselves in a way that allows our natural compassion to flourish. (Marshall Rosenberg, *NonViolent Communication*, p.3)

NVC, also known as 'Compassionate Communication,' is a tool for removing barriers to connection, and building or rebuilding trust and connection. It strives for connection first, solutions later.

Rosenberg's work resonates with Steiner's thoughts on humans as social beings. He delineates the important first step of determining who is listening to whom in the given moment. Am I listening to you, and therefore not having my own spinning of thoughts, just waiting for a break in your speaking to let them out? Am I falling asleep to me and thereby listening to you?

Rudolf Steiner spoke about *Social and Anti-Social Forces in the Human Being* in a lecture in Bern, December 12, 1918. He described that one must 'fall asleep' into the other when truly listening, and be awake when speaking to them.

If we have any kind of relation to other people, or any communication with them, then a force flows between us creating a bond. It is this fact which lies at the basis of social life and which, when broadened, is really the foundation for the social structure of humanity.

One sees this phenomenon most clearly when one thinks of the direct interchange between two people. The impression which one person makes on the other has the effect of lulling the other to sleep. Thus we frequently find in social life that one person gets lulled to sleepiness by the other with whom he has interchange. As a physicist might say: a "latent tendency" is always there for one man to lull another to sleep in social relationships.
Why is this so? Well, we must see that this rests on a very important arrangement of man's total being. It rests on the fact that what we call social impulses, fundamentally speaking, are only present in people of our present day consciousness during sleep... When you know this, you do not need to be surprised when your social being seeks to lull you to sleep in your relationship with others. In the relationship between people the social impulse ought to develop. Yet it can only develop during sleep. Therefore in the relationship between people a tendency is shown for one person to dull the consciousness of the other so that a social relation may be established between them. This

striking fact is evident to one who studies the realities of life. Above all things, our interchange with one another leads to dulling the consciousness of one another, in the interests of a social impulse between people. Of course you cannot go about continually asleep in life. Yet the tendency to establish social impulses consists in, and expresses itself by, an inclination to sleep. That of which I speak goes on subconsciously of course, but it nevertheless actually penetrates our life continuously. Thus there exists a permanent disposition to fall asleep precisely for the building up of the social structure of humanity.

On the other hand, something else is also working. A perpetual struggle and opposition to falling asleep in social relationships is also present. If you meet a person you are continuously standing in a conflict situation in the following way: Because you meet him, the tendency to sleep always develops in you so that you may experience your relationship to him in sleep. But, at the same time, there is aroused in you the counter-force to keep yourself awake. This always happens in the meeting between people — a tendency to fall asleep, a tendency to keep awake. In this situation a tendency to keep awake has an anti-social character, the assertion of one's individuality, of one's personality, in opposition to the social structure of society. Simply because we are human beings, our soul-life swings to and fro between the social and the antisocial. And that which lives in us as these two forces, which may be observed between people communicating, can from an occult perspective be seen to govern our life.

The practice of NVC is an attempt to transform thinking so that there is no more blaming of one's self or the other. Finding fault becomes irrelevant, as does diagnosing wrongness. We can rid ourselves of value judgments (good/bad, labeling,inappropriate/appropriate), making demands, threats and ultimatums. Rosenberg's basic premise is that no one else is responsible for your feelings, they arise in you based on your own needs and values in the context of the particular situation at hand. Connecting to one's own needs and values is a making conscious of personal impulses and motivations for action. It is a path toward knowing yourself, waking up to hidden patterns of reaction and habit. It is a path of awakening to higher levels of will activity (see Steiner, *Study of Man*, lecture 4)

In brief, Rosenberg articulates four levels of human experience connected to a particular situation. First - what happened, what can be observed? It is important to discern the difference between an observation and a label or judgment. Based on one's observation, a feeling arises. Can we discern the difference between a feeling, a true feeling, and a thought? Is 'sad' a feeling? (Yes) Is 'betrayed' a feeling? (No, it's a concept.) There are many pseudo-feelings; thoughts spoken of, and even thought of, as feelings. For instance, "I feel misunderstood." I feel attacked, cheated, mistreated, taken for granted, and so. All of these are NOT feelings, but are thoughts introduced with the false label of 'feeling.' Translated it says' "I think you misunderstand me."

There is a wide range of true human feelings, but they can be grouped and defined as various spectrums of feeling. There is a fascinating description of feelings from an article entitled *What is Restorative Practices?* on the IIRP website articulating the range of true human feelings, or affects. This brief excerpt can be an aid to the understanding of one's own feelings, and can be a compass for understanding others.

S. Tomkins identified nine distinct affects to explain the expression of emotion in all human beings. Most of the affects are defined by pairs of words that represent the least and the most intense expression of a particular affect. The six negative affects include anger-rage, fear-terror, distress-anguish, disgust, dissmell (a word Tomkins coined to describe "turning up one's nose" at someone or something in a rejecting way), and shame-

humiliation. Surprise-startle is the neutral affect, which functions like a reset button. The two positive affects are interest-excitement and enjoyment-joy.

Shame is worthy of special attention. D. Nathanson explains that shame is a critical regulator of human social behavior. Tomkins defined shame as occurring any time that our experience of the positive affects is interrupted (Tomkins, 1987). So an individual does not have to do something wrong to feel shame. The individual just has to experience something that interrupts interest-excitement or enjoyment- joy...

Underlying feelings is the realm of a persons needs, values and intentions. We all have needs, most are universal. Can we discern the difference between needs and expectations? On this level, as soon as we are thinking someone else should have, or shouldn't have done or said something, we are operating from an expectation. When blame is placed on another person for our own negative feelings, we are not connected to our own true need. And when we come to the stage of doing something about it, can we discern the difference between making a request (they can say yes or no) or a demand (they have no choice) on another person? Connecting with own feelings and needs is key to the path of know thyself. The more connected one is with their own feelings and needs, the potential is greater for connecting, true connecting with the other.

A basic principle of NVC is that we all share the same needs, they are universal. What differs is the strategies we individually create to get our needs met, and how we prioritize our needs, our own personal hierarchy of needs. All of our actions are motivated by the attempt, conscious or not, to meet needs. Anything and everything anyone does is to meet a need. *All our actions are attempts to meet our needs.*

One can thereby see the importance of becoming conscious of this soul level in ourselves. If we can understand our needs, as well as our personal habitual strategies for meeting those needs, we are striving on the path of knowing ourself.

Marshall Rosenberg also points to the importance of communicating needs and requests to someone else in forty words or less. *40 words or less.* If you go on longer, your audience tunes out. He is referring to 40 words or less when communicating needs and requests to grown-ups. So, with a young child, I think it works best in one quarter of that. 10 words or less to communicate your needs and request to a young child!

Non Violent Communication teaches a process languaging in which the intent is to connect and create mutual understanding. It is a life serving process that connects to what is alive in the moment for the human beings interacting. I think of it as practical applied anthroposophy in that it develops a thinking and speaking from the heart that enables connection between human beings. It is a practical path toward true empathy.

I highly recommend looking into Non Violent Communication as part of an adult path of self development. Surely there is a practitioner or trainer in your area from whom you can glean the basics. (The NVC website is www.cnvc.org.) As always, keep the development of consciousness of the child central in your thinking if and when you decide to apply these practices in your life and work with young children. Consideration of the consciousness of the child has to determine how one utilizes this style of communication practice with young children. Young children don't yet have the capacities for negotiation, and the abstract thinking required for understanding their own feelings, needs and intentions. With young children, one must find their own way to practicing NVC. In my kindergarten, and other interactions with young children, I have taken up NVC in my own unique way, as we all must.

When I reveal to the children what my needs are in a situation, I make myself vulnerable. That means I remove barriers to seeing into me, the real me, and there is an immediate and direct connection possible. The children can honor what my need is because the situation has been reframed. For example, several children, ages five and six, are stacking chairs intending to climb up to the top – four chairs high. I say, "In kindergarten, two is as high as we go."

"But whyyyyy?," whines one. "Yeah," says another. "It is important to me that everyone is safe. Two is all," I reply. And they take down the higher chairs, and don't attempt to build that high for the remainder of the school year. Really!
I have trained myself to tell the children what I like and what I don't like. This is my truth in a situation. It is never 'bad,' or 'inappropriate,' or 'wrong' to do a particular action. These words are completely subjective and have no intrinsic reality. There is no way to make objective determinations of those concepts. Good for one can be bad for another. Right in this situation can be wrong in another for another person. But I can know if I like or don't like something. And when I make it a practice to speak from that place of truth, the children through imitation begin to let each other know when someone does something that another doesn't like. And then it comes from a place of truth, "This is how this really affects me," and is respected and responded to as such *by the other children.*

None of the preceding is intended as a script or recipe of any kind. I merely am offering examples of what I might say, and my own thinking behind it. You will have to find your own way. As it is said; "You can't whistle with another man's mouth."

We are in a position of great responsibility. One of our tasks as teachers and parents of young children is to become fully conscious of our speech and language, so that the children are supported in awakening at their own pace in a healthy way, and so that out of imitation they develop tools for communicating that actually support connection. Early childhood is so precious and passes so quickly; we should cherish these special years and not rush them by.

SL- "It's over. The quest. We have found the promised Word, the Word whose existence was whispered to us by the whirling dervish all those years ago......We've found the grail...Language is what hides it. Language limits us to approximations. How can I communicate the ineffable except by trusting that you know what I mean? Don't you see? The fall of humanity was the fall from the actual to the symbolic. Language abstracts us from the real world, keeping us from direct, intuitive perception. Words, like the ego [as in 'egoism'], are merely guides. Don't mistake them for the real thing...Language makes an enigma of simple existence, it obscures the true nature of reality, and of your Self.
RH- What am I to do?
SL- Just be your Self. Don't put your ego where it doesn't belong. Your ego is a tool to assist you in life. Don't mistake it for who you are. The ego is a distracting backseat driver who thinks it knows everything. Keep it in its proper place. Tape its mouth shut, so you can better enjoy the ride instead of trying to control it....." (Tony Vigorito , *Just a Couple of Days*, p. 363)

Chapter 6

Conflict Resolving with Young Children: A Short Guide for Getting Beyond Shame and Blame and Premature Abstract Thinking

Children must be educated by love, not by punishment.
James Joyce

Often young children engage in activities that the adult is not happy about, that seems not safe, or not healthy. Then the adult has a great opportunity to teach by example. The first response of the adult sets the tone for rest of the interaction to come. If the adult can maintain her calm and centeredness, then she is in a position to choose her response, rather than react. This quality of calm responding is an essential soul characteristic for the continuing sanity of an early childhood educator or parent. When the adult is able to respond and not react, the child experiences positive leadership from the adult, and takes this deeply into his developing will through imitation.

Understanding the particular developmental stage of the child's consciousness is essential in navigating challenging situations. Adults need qualities of patience and persistence when meeting the young child, because the young child is not quick to adopt changes in his behavior. You may have to repeat yourself a number of times. The child may do the unwanted behavior again and again, even after you have tried to bring a change. The child may not respond as quickly as you would, or as quickly as you would like. Therefore the development of patience and persistence for the adult are crucial if the adult intends to maintain their own calm.

Another critical factor in creating and maintaing a harmonious environment is the adult's awareness of the particular child's needs for rest and food. Each of of us has a unique rate of metabolizing food, and when we as adults ensure that the child maintains sufficient fueling so many conflicts are avoided. The same is true for rest. Crankiness and conflicts often arise simply because the child (or the adult) is tired or hungry, so creating a suitable rhythm of eating and rest, and keeping to it, is an important factor in smooth flowing life with young children.

Since the child's primary learning mode is imitation, we must remember that it is our doing and our speaking that will be imitated, and through that imitation the young child will learn. Instructing a young child simply is not effective, nor does it support their development! Keep in mind that when there is some behavior a child engages in that you would like him not to do, the longer you 'let it slide' the harder it becomes to change or eliminate later. And it might require many, many interventions of the same kind to bring the change you desire. Responding early and *often* is called for, but in a manner that is true and effective, as we will see in this chapter.

The use of shame and blame techniques are widespread for interacting with young children to get them to do what is wanted. Punishment, coercion, threats and bribes are used to motivate behavior, or to attempt to prevent future behaviors. Ordering, demanding and nagging are widespread techniques for getting children (or anyone) to do what is wanted.

Young children learn by imitation! I keep repeating this because it is so crucial to keep in mind. This imitation goes deeply into the child's developing soul patterning creating reaction habits that will be life long. Is it desirable for a child to grow up with the unconscious reaction patterns of shame and blame? Do we want children to become adults who rely on rewards and punishments to motivate others? Again we have to look at the question of carrot or stick in our selves.

"How could you do that to him?" Scolding, threatening, and moralizing don't work, nor do lecturing, explaining and reasoning. "Don't, don't, don't..." is too often what the children hear. As mentioned in the previous chapter, words like 'right' and 'wrong,' 'appropriate' and 'not appropriate,' 'good' and 'bad,' are relative terms and completely subjective. Those words have no inherent, objective truth. It is perfectly natural and sensible for a child to take what he wants from another, or try any method possible, perhaps even hitting to get it. Is that bad? Wrong? The child is simply using a strategy to get what he wants. The fact is that someone else doesn't like it. And that is a fact, the only pertinent fact. Something's wrongness or badness is purely subjective and perspective based. In situations where something has happened that we didn't want to happen, or don't like what happened, the truest thing to say is, "I don't like that," or, "Johnny didn't like that." That is objective truth. The children are learning values from the adults through imitation, and those values shine forth when we speak the truth from our heart. When we express how the action affects us directly, or how it affected another child, we are transmitting objective truth instead of a judgment.

"In kindergarten we use our words." This is a wonderful mantra likely needing to be repeated over and over and over. Eventually it becomes true, and eventually it rays out beyond kindergarten into home life, and other settings. Speaking can be considered as a sort of protection because if the speaking continues, physical violence doesn't arise. Though speaking can be violent and aggressive, it still is not physical aggression. If people were able to speak about their frustrations and problems, verbal and physical violence could be averted. Human beings, and even young children, can learn to ask for something, to make requests, and out of connecting and creativity, solutions can be found.

Through example, adults can teach verbal habits that are tools for the children to resolve their own conflicts. Of course one must respond to the situation in the moment with directness and brevity and not meet the young child in an intellectual and abstract manner. Here's an example from kindergarten:

Jack was playing with a small wooden boat. Jill approached Jack and took the boat and went to another part of the room to play with the boat. Perhaps Jack was pushed, but I did not see that for myself. Jack cried. Jill played.

There are many possible approaches for a teacher to take. For example; "Jill! Give that back to Jack and say you are sorry." Or; "Jill. How do you think Jack feels? What would you feel like if he did that to you?"

The adult's approach must be specific for the particular children involved and the particular situation. Always central in my thinking is what is the consciousness of the child. We cannot expect the young child to be able to understand how someone else is feeling, when she is just beginning to be able to label her own feelings. Also, to simply require an apology ("Go tell him you're sorry.") does not allow Jill to help resolve the situation herself – she doesn't learn anything. Learning requires the will to be engaged, and requiring an apology does not involve the child's own will. Lastly, it is important not to blame one of the children or to make them "wrong." I wouldn't say, "You hurt him." Or "You know better. You should feel ashamed of yourself." "How could you?" I try to meet each child with a true attitude of love and openness to their own needs. Shaming and blaming habits so deeply permeate our culture, even already into the tender souls of young children. I have observed time and again when practicing this style of restoring peace and harmony, early in the school year many children immediately flinch, drop their heads and hunch their shoulders in typical response patterns to trauma. It is as if they are physically readying themselves for the heaping of shame and blame about to fall on them. You can see it in their body's gestures, and it saddens me to see. I want to be able to care for the children in a situation without anyone feeling like they are about to be blamed or shamed.

Perhaps I would say, "He is hurt and needs some care." Or, to Jill with my hand outstretched and open, palm up; "It is Jack's turn now and you may have a turn next." Or, to Jill "Jack is sad. Can you do something that will help him?" The children know what would be a help for each other, and they simply need an opportunity to activate this compassionate activity. It is important to have a sense of the particular child, and his stage of consciousness development. For some children, I might look around the room, not at all in the direction of the child whose action led to the sadness of the other, and say, "What can we do to help Jack?" For some children, I might look straight in the eyes and say, "What can you do to help Jack?" This gives the children a chance to engage their own will in an act of helping and compassion.

We have spoken often about the child's natural trust in the world and people as the basis for imitation, and a need for a secure sense of the world as a good place. Conflict situations are breakdowns in trust and connection. Resolving conflicts needs to be a restoration of essential trust and connection thereby allowing the child to resume his dream-like exploration of the natural and social worlds. The best technique when adult intervention is necessary is to use words that you would be happy if the children had said themselves, and if they took up those phrases through imitation. Give them phrases that are direct, non-blaming, true and succinct so that in future situations, those phrases are the tools in their social tool box. When those phrases become habits, you have succeeded.

When the adult is active in the use of verbal tools worthy of imitation and practices compassion for the one hurt, the children develop communication tools for their social life, and conflicts are resolved more easily. The children begin to imitate a non-blaming way of resolving their own conflicts and more and more peace descends into their life, into the kindergarten, and the world. These seeds planted in early childhood bear fruit later as capacities for checking in with one's own needs and the needs of the other, and finding solutions where the needs of both can be met.

Carrot and Stick

One widespread habit of interacting with young children is through punishment, coercion, bribes and threats; all varieties of carrot or stick approaches. These are techniques of using power over another person. All of these are based on the assumption of an adversarial relationship. Is that the sort of relationship teachers or parents want with children? There certainly are times when we would have the children do differently than what they are doing. There are times when we would like to influence the children to act in a certain way. The children will internalize the motivation techniques of the adult. What style of social motivation do we want the children to imitate in their own interactions? This use of power to get what we want is deeply unconscious in us, and is learned from parents, loved ones and care providers at a very early age. It is difficult for the adult to become aware of how she attempts to use power over others as a tool, yet it is well worth the personal inner exploration of this as part of one's path of self discovery and self development. (See chapter 7). Rewards and punishments are two sides of the same coin, and neither is the type of motivation that I value. I want to develop inner habits of social responsibility and listening that will not arise from use of motivation techniques using power.

When something happens that is different than the adult wants there are various approaches to take. The traditional *punitive* approach starts with finding out what happened and who did it. Then the adult decides how they will be punished?

An alternative could be called a *unitive* approach. Still there is a need to find out what happened, hopefully with little to no questioning and probing. Ideally the adult saw it happen. And also knows who was affected. Then the consideration is given to what can be done to make things right again?

I often will say to five and six-year-olds something like, "Susie is sad. What can we do to help her?" in full expectation that the child who took what Susie was playing with will give it back. Again it so depends on knowing the two children involved. Sometimes I look above the heads of the group of children when asking, "What can we do to help?" Sometimes I may look directly at the child who I saw take the toy when asking the very same question. And every once in a while I even look directly at the child who I saw take the toy and ask, "What can *you* do to help Susie?" It all depends on my understanding each of the children and their own particular stage of development.

Often adults have hidden reaction patterns developed in their early childhood that want retaliation for wrongs done. The need to retaliate is the opposite of awareness and letting go.

It is a healthy idea to take a serious look at yourself and see if you are a "carrot" or a "stick" person, or a little bit of both. Is this how you would consciously choose to help change the actions of another person?

We can present a positive alternative to the action we saw in simple words, accompanied by actions. It works best to verbalize what we want instead of what we don't. Rather than "Don't run inside. You might fall and hurt yourself," say, "We walk inside, we run outside." Instead of "Don't slam the door. It's too loud," try, "We close the door gently," in a quiet voice while demonstrating. "Hands are for work and play and taking care of others," while gently stroking the hands that have hit, is a favorite of mine. If a child uses a stick for poking another child, for instance, I can say, "This stick needs a rest now." If two children are squabbling over a toy and aren't able to resolve it themselves, I make a decision and say, "Sally may have a turn now, and Mary will have a turn next." Important to keep in mind is that young children are not naughty or bad! Their actions are not good or bad, or wrong. They are adventurers and explorers searching for their way in the physical and social world. They are looking for strategies that are successful in attaining their goals. The strategy of taking the toy you want from another child can be a successful strategy. At the same time, it might be a strategy the other child doesn't like. Is the strategy 'inappropriate?' Is the behavior 'bad?' What is true is the other person involved did not like the action, and perhaps you as adult do not like the action. But it is merely a strategy that will continue to be used until the adults support another habit of getting needs met to emerge for the child. Our job is to guide and lead them on their path with our actions and words, as a living example of a way we would like to see people interact.

Sometimes in their play a group of children might tell one child he can't play with them, and the left out child is sad. Whether he comes to me and says," They won't let me play," or I observe it myself, this situation receives my intervention. I walk over to the group and say, "Jack wants to play too." Often that is all it takes. Sometimes, "But our house is too small." "I respond, "I'll help you make it bigger." Eventually, the children can carry on these interactions without me. How long it takes depends on the particular children.

Sometimes a child wants to play alone, and then might tell another child they don't want anyone else to play. Solitary playtime is needed by some children so I do allow it when it is one child playing by him or herself. Sometimes though, it is two children who say, "We want to play alone," while telling another he can't join in. I respond, "We don't leave anyone out in kindergarten."

It may happen that Jack and Jill are having some sort of dispute. Jack then says to Jill, "You are a dodo-head." I say, "Her name is Jill and that is what we will call her. Or, "You will call her Jill. In kindergarten we use each other's true names."

An oft-heard phrase, when telling someone they are not part of the 'group,' is, "Well, you can't come to my birthday party." I say, "In kindergarten we only talk about parties that everyone is invited to.

I want the children to use words of kindness toward each other, and to refrain from telling everyone in earshot what they hate. A visitor to my kindergarten would hear me saying time and again phrases such as, "We use kind words in kindergarten," and what my own father used to say, "If you don't have anything nice to say, don't say anything at all." In fact, numerous times I have said, "My father used to say this, "If you don't have anything nice to say…""

It's lunchtime in kindergarten, and four-year-old Daisy is talking with food in her mouth again. I say, "I can't understand your words. Chew and swallow first, and then talk."

In the springtime, when the flowers start to bloom, little fingers just itch to pick them. At my kindergarten there are 'picking flowers' that are available to be picked at anytime, and for the most part bloom year-round. There are also 'not picking' flowers, about which I say a mantra over and over, "These flowers are for everyone to look at," followed by, "You can pick those flowers, there."

It is meal time and we are singing our blessing song of gratitude and reverence. Only two boys are singing in a falsetto voice and replacing the words with other less reverent ones. I stop mid-song, without even a glance toward the two operatic singers, and say, "I like to hear everyone's true voices." And we start over, and this time everyone sings without the making fun the previous rendition was having.

In the Grimm's story *The Queen Bee*, Simpleton, the youngest of the three brothers, says, in three different situations, "Leave the creatures in peace. I will not suffer you to harm them." For the last few years, I have told this story early in the kindergarten year when the group dynamic and chemistry is beginning to reveal itself. Then when various situations arise, I have something to work with. At playtime, Ian and Bobby are cheetahs and they are hunting for rabbits (Three girls are playing that they are rabbits.) The cheetahs are growling and snapping their teeth at the rabbits. I say, "Leave the creatures in peace." The phrase has a context because I have already told the story, and the children respond by cheetahs going away and finding some other lunch, several logs that are pieces of meat.

Occasionally, it is too late for leaving the creatures in peace. Even with the best of supervision, it sometimes happens that a child hits another. If I have seen it, I say, "You will not hit. Everyone needs to be safe here." Or perhaps, "There is no hitting here," and taking the child's hands gently in mine, "Hands are for work and hands are for play and hands are for taking care of others.It is so important to keep in mind that children are exploring and discovering all the time. And because of their stage of consciousness development, they are self centered, even though they are not completely connected with their own self. If a young child sees something interesting to him, he healthfully and naturally will want to pick it up and examine and play with it, even if someone else already is playing with it. Is something wrong with his action? No. Can he understand at age three that picking it up might make someone else sad or angry? No.

Perhaps three-year-old Mikey picks up a handful of sand, and I see him prepare to throw it in the direction of some other children. While scooping Mikey up in my arms, I say, "We will not throw sand. The sand stays on the ground." And then I set him down outside the sand area, well aware that I might have to repeat this any number of times on many days to come. For the two- and three-year-olds, it is important to deliver the boundary a the most direct way, simply by saying "No."

"No. You will not hit." And perhaps follow up with "Hands are for work, and hands are for play, and hands are for taking care of others." Or, "No. You will not bite him. Everyone needs to be safe." The two and three-year olds are even more in their will, and less in their self-awareness, so presenting boundaries in the physical realm is extra important. And it takes repetition! We are trying to develop habits, trying to make the physical/social boundaries become habits. Try not to be discouraged or frustrated when the child is again repeating the unwanted behavior. Persistence, patience and calmness will get you through.

I read a funny anecdote about a woman who had asked Dr. Steiner what to do about her young child who spit a lot. Steiner told her that by the time the boy was thirty years old, he wouldn't be doing it anymore, so she should try not to worry about it.

In my kindergarten (and in my home when my own children were young) there is a hard and fast boundary about weapons that shoot, even pretend, invisible ones. "We don't play shooting games in kindergarten," is another oft-repeated phrase, especially at the beginning of a school year. "Guns are not welcome here." Children are very creative, and the gun is immediately transformed, "It just shoots fire." Me again, "There are no shooting games in kindergarten." No bombs, no blowing things up, and not even in their drawings (unless there seems to be a specific pedagogical therapeutic need). I do let the children play with 'swords,' though as soon as a 'sword' is pointed at a real person or animal, the sword (stick) is having a rest. This is my personal boundary, my own value. You will have to decide for yourself what to do in the realm of weapons play.

It is important to find a balance with the adult use of the word 'no.' Some young children hear it far to often, as described earlier, and some adults avoid 'no' as a response to young children altogether. "No' is a powerful word when you mean it, and especially for young children, it can be an aid in helping them toward social boundaries. The three year old boy who has just picked up a handful of sand and is about to throw it, from one foot away, at another child's face needs to be told, "No, we don't throw sand." This is a safety concern for the other child, and needs immediate intervention by the adult. When the word 'no' is administered with calm firmness and with awareness of the child's need to have safe boundaries, it helps the child develop a secure sense of self.

When the five year old girl is in the loft, above the other children, and has a log teetering on the edge, and she is nudging it to fall, "No, the log stays away from the edge!"

If 'no' was used, then it is always useful to give the child a suggestion about what they CAN do, "The log stays away from the edge." "Sand stays on the ground." 'No' is an important tool for creating safe boundaries in the physical and social realm.

Okay, so you have already said to the five-year-old in the loft that logs stay away from the edge. And there it is again, teetering, being nudged again toward the edge and the unsuspecting children below. I like to respond with, "Steve said logs stay away from the edge." I refer to myself in the third person rather than create a direct confrontation with the child such, "I said …" It is a softer response for the child to take in, and it is likely that many behavioral safety issues we bring up with the children will need to be repeated again and again. This way makes it easier for the adult and the child not to take it personally and to simply get on with pushing the log away from the edge again. If I refer to something I have said as in the third person, it is made objective. It is no longer a conflict between the child and me; I am merely repeating something that has already been spoken, albeit by me. It is a just a fact that we can't argue about - "Steve said..." - and it serves as a effective reminder without adding conflict. "Oh, Steve did say that.

Often there are actions you want the child to take, but he or she is not noticing what is yet undone, or is not participating. Coming in from outside, I see a jacket left on a bench. I know who it belongs to, and rather than naming the child and telling her to go get it, I say, "There is one jacket left outside." It brings to the child's attention that something is left undone, and the action wanting to happen speaks for itself. And the child who may not have noticed checks for her jacket and discovers it is the one left out. Out of her will, she collects her jacket and hangs it inside. My words of observation were a stimulus for the child's will response.

Perhaps it is tidy-away time in kindergarten, and a child is standing empty-handed, not participating in putting things away, and you want him to help. Sometimes i make a spoken observation like, "Over there is a cloth." Sometimes all it takes to bring the child's will into activity is for their attention to be brought to something that needs to be done, without telling them to do it. Their own will takes care of that.

I might pick up a log, walk toward the child who is simply standing without helping, and hand him the log. He takes it, and I walk on, not having said anything. He is now holding a log, his will engages, and he puts it on the shelf, and then joins in the tidying away. Or several children have made a restaurant at playtime, and you want them to help out things away. They are still at it; taking orders and cooking food. I pick up a plate and spoon and say, "Here is the food Sally wanted at the dishes store." And the child delivers the order to the shelf where the cooking toys are put away.Or, folding up various colored cloths, I say, "I need someone to deliver this cherry pie (the red cloth)."A child presents herself for delivery, and takes the 'pie' to the shelf where it belongs. Other children come to help put them away because I have made a blueberry pie, lime pie, strawberry, and so on. I have entered into the land of imagination where the children live, and for many young children, this can be an instant cure for 'the not-helping-at-tidy-away-time syndrome.

"Take these boards to the lumber store." "These [wooden] animals go to the zoo." You get the idea. It is important also for the adult to be part of the task, rather than assigning it to the children. If the reality is 'we are tidying up' it is far more effective than saying to the child or children, "you tidy this up."

One phrase I have heard used by adults toward young children, and used to use myself, is "You may…" when the adult really means "You must…" On the one hand it sounds like the adult is giving the child permission to do the desired (by the adult) action, but the adult is actually inwardly and with his tone demanding the child obey. "You may put that stick down." Translation, "You have to put that stick down." When you speak the words "You may…," it sounds like you are offering a choice. You have permission to do this if you choose. When speaking to the young child, the intent needs to match the words chosen. One could instead say, "You will put that stick down. The stick needs a rest." If I am saying something in which I am not offering a choice whether to do or not, I prefer to say, "You will…"

When my stepson Michael was in Rosie's Waldorf kindergarten, he and his best friend Brendan would fight, kick each other, bite each other, and various other physical attacks on each other. They both would end up crying. At pick-up time they still would both want to go to each other's house to play after kindergarten. One day Rosie asked Michael why he was doing all those things to Brendan. He answered, "I don't do it. My bones do it." Michael was aware that he, when connected to his self controlled aspect, wouldn't have done it, and therefore didn't do it. He also was aware, remarkably, that his body was engaged in those activities. For me this explains how a child whom you observed hit another, responds when you ask about it, "I didn't do it." In the moment their bodies do things, their reactions kick in, but when asked about, it is clear to them that their self would not have and therefore did not participate in the actions.

There are times when a child seems unable to engage in play successfully with the other children. Perhaps he is being argumentative, or rather than building houses, he is knocking them down, and snatching things form others. It happens. One magical tool for turning that sort of behavior around is work, real, meaningful work. When the child is engaged in sanding the boards, or cutting the vegetables, or sweeping the floor *with the adult*, after a time he suddenly relaxes and says, "Can I go play now?" You know that he is ready again to enter the world of social play. The working engaged his will and allowed his thinking to drift until he truly was ready to –re-engage in play. It is much more helpful if he is working next to a grown-up who has his will engaged – this example for the child's will is powerful. Also, children in the nearly 6 – year old range often are in a transition in their thinking, in their play. The younger ones are full of the fantasy that is speaking to them from the world all the time. The older ones, six-ish, are transitioning to inner imagining in their play. The transition is not sudden and total, it is gradual and stop/start. Sometimes they experience lulls, and this is often when they are at a loss in how to play. This is when work is so valuable because they are at a stage when they can become quite skillful, as well as helping them to relax back into play.

Time-out is a popular technique some adults employ for behavior modification. When a time-out is used, usually the adult first demands that the child stop whatever behavior it is that the adult is finding unpleasant. The child is told to stop the misbehaving and be quiet. When the child doesn't stop, he is required to go and sit alone somewhere, away from the adults and other children, and told not to get up until he can better control himself.

What has led to this situation? In most cases it is that the child has become upset and demanding when their needs were not met. As mentioned earlier, all behaviors is based on attempting to meet needs. Young children lack the ability to meet their own needs, in trust they depend on adults to make sure their needs are met. Rest, food, warmth, safety in play situations, etc… all are needs that adults must see to for the young child. Additionally, young children tolerate frustration even less well than adults, and are less likely to be able to identify their own frustrated need that is upsetting them.

Being put in a time-out prolongs the time that a child feels upset about their frustrated need that stimulated their 'misbehavior.' What exacerbates this increasingly uncomfortable state of being frustrated is the fact that the child is alone, away from the adults who they rely on for meeting their needs. Separation from the trusted adult, a main source of comfort and security, adds to the challenge of the situation for a child. The child feels this as punishment.

Moreover, being alone in time-out can lead to feelings of fear and anxiety. Being alone and in time-out increases the frustrations felt by a child who is already feeling frustrated. For the frustrated and uncomfortable child, time-out offers enforced silence and the need to squash whatever feeling he was having that led to the time-out. Time-out tells a child that uncomfortable emotions need to be ignored and denied in himself. Children learn to ignore their feelings of hurt and anger. They learn to repress their painful feelings. In some children, nervous habits arise to distract them form their uncomfortable feelings such as nail biting and thumb sucking. As a result, being unaware of feelings can often become a habit for the child as he grows into adulthood.

Sometimes I do employ the 'other room' for pedagogical practices. Sita has a very loud voice. In my kindergarten, we use 'inside voices' when we are inside. Sita often forgets, so occasionally I say, "Sita, go on into the coatroom and find your inside voice." She happily goes in there, and comes back when she has found her inside voice and is speaking more quietly, at least for a little while.

At other times I have asked children to go into the coatroom and find their 'walking feet,' since we walk inside. It is NOT time-out. It is a chance for the child to re-enter the kindergarten with at least a momentary awareness of the social boundary I am trying to develop and maintain in them, and eventually it does become the habit to speak more softly and walk inside. Boundaries create a feeling of safety and protection for child, and nurture development of self reliance.

Sometimes children repeatedly go to find one or another forgotten item in the coatroom. And they come back on their own time and of their own accord. My coatroom is a special place where children can go to find many things including their "listening ears,' their "inside voices," their walking feet," and their "peaceful playing." Ian was particularly loud one day. I said he could go into the coatroom to find his inside voice. He said, "And I think I know just where it is."

If the children's voices are louder than you prefer, there are many ways to attempt to lower the volume. "Shhh (a very brisk airy sound). That is too loud." *Shh* is one of the fire sounds; it has a stinging and harsh quality. *Shh* is the sort of sound you might use in a theater if someone was talking during the show, but not with a child. I would rather the children not take up the habit of 'shushing' each other when the volume is louder than they like. "Be quiet," also does not sit well with me. My favorite method is to silently put one index finger to my lips while pursing my lips. It usually works wonders with the children four years and older. Sometimes I'll accompany the finger-to-lips gesture with "The voices are so loud," or, "Inside voices." I try to say 'so loud' rather than 'too loud' because how could I know what decibel level is 'too' loud.

Several three year olds are playing. They are wolves, hunting for food and howling. The howling is louder than I like so I sing in a simple improvised pentatonic melody, "Quiet voices in the house," or "Howling is for outside." One child responds, "But we are wolves." I reply, "And even wolves howl quietly inside their house." For the younger children especially, using a singing voice to both get their attention and to deliver the message can be very effective. Their 'dream' consciousness is an especially musical reality and singing often is noticed while speaking might not be.

It can help to be aware of the individual reaction patterns of the children in your care. This can eliminate the surprise element and perhaps avoid switching on your own reactive pattern.
The following description of shame responses has helped me be more empathic and less reactive with the children. In the previous chapter we noted that shame occurs any time that experience of the positive feelings are interrupted. So an individual does not have to be reprimanded to feel shame. He simply has to experience an interruption of the positive feeling spectrums of either interest-excitement or enjoyment- joy.

D. Nathanson (http://www.iirp.org/whatisrp.php) *has developed the compass of shame to illustrate the various ways that human beings react when they feel shame. The four poles of the compass of shame and behaviors associated with them are:*
Withdrawal — isolating oneself, running and hiding; Attack self — self put-down, masochism; Avoidance — denial, abusing drugs, distraction through thrill seeking; Attack others — turning the tables, lashing out verbally or physically, blaming others. Nathanson says that the "attack other" response to shame is responsible for the proliferation of violence in modern life. (from *What is Restorative Practices?*)

If we can become more aware of these possible results of interrupted fun, we can be more understanding of the children's reactions, and more prepared for what might happen.

Adult awareness of the possible effects of changes in rhythm can alleviate some stress and tension in the adult. When it is the first day back to kindergarten after a holiday break, there is often more chaos and a resurgence of behaviors you thought were gone.

When a new child is added to the group mid year, when it's windy or rain is imminent the chaos level automatically rises as does the quantity of challenging social situations for the children. If the adult is inwardly prepared for these changes, she has a calmer attitude in responding to them

Humor

Don't underestimate the power and magic of humor. Levity can take all the charge out of a heated situation. Silliness can go a long way to reduce conflict and help move things forward. So keep a healthy supply of humor up your sleeve for whatever might arise.

In my kindergarten we have a circle time everyday of songs and poems sung and spoken together and acted out. I have given a lot of planning and memorizing and practice as preparation for doing it with the children. It is possible that I become invested in the idea of the children following merrily along. I could develop an expectation that they will cooperatively imitate me. And it is possible that one or another child will not participate the way I want them to, perhaps even being distracting to the others and disruptive to our having circle time. What to do?

I always want to have some options, some variations to what I have planned available 'up my sleeve' for any contingency.

Changing the movements I use with a particular poem, or adding in a new song usually is all it takes to bring back a certain harmony and group participation at circle time.

For both circle time and story time, a powerful tool for allowing the child to enter into the imaginations we are offering is the inner strength of focus of the adult. If one is mentally picturing the images of the story, if one is vividly imagining the pictures that arise from the songs and poems, then the children are much more likely to stay with your imagination. The will of the adult is a powerful force stimulating imitation of the young child, and if the adult is actively willing their thinking, the child can relax and live into the imagination of the mental pictures the adult is speaking. The children are creating their own pictures inwardly, and it helps if they are imitating an adult doing the same activity. The kindergarten teacher as storyteller or circle time leader must inwardly "see" the pictures for those activities to come alive for the children.

I practice social engineering as a means or conflict reduction. Who do I think would do well sitting beside whom? Who do I want to be near to me or my assistant? Having regular assigned seating at meal times and story time eliminates many conflicts. There is no more, "I don't want to sit next to her," or disputes about who gets to sit beside the teacher.

The key to avoidance of most 'conflict situations is to be aware of the children's developmental stages and their needs, and be proactive in ensuring those needs are met. Plan, and plan ahead! I mentioned this earlier in this chapter - the daily rhythm of meal times, and rest times, and so on, eliminates so much conflict. The child's growing body has a huge need for nutrition and rest, and caring for these needs is the adult's responsibility. Consistently and rhythmically meeting the child's needs for nourishment, rest, exercise, play, warmth and attention eliminates most conflicts and allows the child to be in the moment, where they belong.

The most important thing is to establish an education through which human beings learn once more how to live with one another. (Rudolf Steiner, *The Younger Generation,* p. 149/150)

Chapter 7

On the Self Development of the Adult

Self education is a moral question – Have I a right to educate the child unless I educate myself?
Margret Meyerkort

A proper seeking of the spirit exists only when people want to understand the spirit, only when they love the spirit that is active in themselves. It exists only when people can form a bridge between the spiritual reality in themselves and the spiritual reality in the world. Only through such a spirit and through the knowledge of such a spirit can we develop the social pedagogical strength that we need for human life now and in the near future.

Thus, we can only repeat time and again:

May the dark unconscious desires living in human hearts and minds flame up into the conscious life of soul, so that humanity may find, in this age when social concern has become so bright, the true spiritual power of the world with which inner spiritual powers of humans can connect. Out of this union between the World Spirit and the human spirit will flow the best source of social pedagogical strength for human life.
(R. Steiner, 11/25/1919, Basel)

There are certain soul qualities that are helpful, in fact, essential to develop for anyone who spends significant time with young children. These qualities include patience and persistence, calmness, thinking ahead, intuition, and imagination. Also necessary is a foundation of inspiration to motivate your own development. The striving to attain these soul characteristics is an effort of will that serves to educate yourself, as well as working on the will of the children

Imitation is not only about behavior. Imitation penetrates into and forms the physical body (the organs) and can strengthen the life forces by creating healthy habits. Our attempting to lead ourselves toward being truly human has significant impact on the child. Our striving for self-development is worth imitating. *Become what you want the change to be.* Then the activity of the adult in striving to develop new capacities penetrates deeply into the developing child and can bear fruit much later in the child's life. Therefore the central task of the adult becomes an attempt to make oneself worthy of imitation. The first step is becoming aware of our selves in all respects. For example: Where does my body hold tension? Am I awake in my speaking? What are my reaction patterns? How do I walk? ...and so on... All of these and more are worthy of serious self study.

The main question is that of relating; the tool is one's self. A core principle for me is the meeting of the other, and to truly meet the other, be it a child or anyone else, one must first know thyself. How connected are we with our own self? *Know Thyself* is the motto of the ancient mystery centers, and this must become our guiding intention as well.

Daily Review

One exercise that is especially helpful is what Rudolf Steiner called *Ruckshau*, a looking back over the day. This involves a daily review at the end of one's day, starting with the moment just before bed, and going backwards through the day until first awakening that morning. Steiner suggested that one could do this in about five minutes, that it is a quick review just having a brief glance at the various events of the day. The body is relaxed and the thinking is active in picturing the events of the day in backwards order. It provides an opportunity to observe yourself, and discover your 'trigger points.' In going backwards, you might notice a moment when you are all worked up about something, and slowly go back a bit until you notice the moment when your 'button was pushed.' This is NOT an exercise in self-judgment. It is a way to discover your own patterns of reaction and perhaps after observing the same pattern time and again in the daily review, one time you might have a spark of awareness in the midst of your day while about to react habitually. "Oh, here I am in a situation where I usually get triggered. How do I want to respond this time?" It might be fleeting, but eventually lasting awareness of your soul habits is created and therefore the opportunity for changing those habits arises. First you see your habits, then you have the possibility of changing them.

Practice of this exercise can help develop the awareness to discover what are your judgments, reactions, feelings, desires, expectations and more. This review exercise also serves as an opportunity to observe whether one is a carrot or stick wielder.

Look again and again at yourself with honesty in this daily practice. Try and find your trigger points, to know your self better and better, and see the patterns of reacting, your personal 'buttons.' This exercise also allows us to develop compassion and kindness for our self for our shortcomings. *Can I feel tenderness and compassion for the very faults and weaknesses that I am struggling with?*

As adults caring for young children, we must become able to be aware of ourselves in the moment, and aware of what the children are doing and saying - awareness of both at once!

Developing Observation Capacity

Above, in the half-open door, Rudolf Steiner stood, having just said good-bye to another visitor, and watched most carefully as I slowly came up the stairs. I have never seen anyone as observant as he was. It was as if - quite immobile, given up selflessly – he let one create oneself again, as it were, in a subtle element in his own soul, which he offered up for that purpose. It was not a matter of thinking about the other, more an inner re-creation in mind and spirit in which the whole growth and development of the other would be revealed. (Friedrich Rittlemeyer, in *The Therapeutic Eye* by Peter Selg, p.11)

One quality worthy of development in a teacher or parent is the capacity for truly observing, and it can be a doorway to deep connecting with another person. First is to learn to separate true observation from opinions, interpretations, labels and judgments. What do the phenomena say? Pretend you have a video camera – all it can record are what is visible and what is audible. That is the full range of observation - anything more is your own add-on. It can be helpful to practice observation exercises in nature, not with human beings at first. Write down your observations, and then review what you have written. Eliminate where you have labeled or judged. Scratch out interpretations you made. Erase thoughts about the observation. If you keep at it, you will develop a sense for what is truly observation. Truly observing is a path to the spiritual activity that lies behind the created world. Practicing observing nature starts to unveil the activity of the spiritual world. By observing nature, one can begin to see the creative powers at work, the spiritual activity that is continuously creating the physical world. To see the creative forces standing behind the physical we need both practice observing nature and a meditative practice.

We are trying to develop the capacity for noticing the details of how the child walks, the shape of his ears, eyes, nose and hands. Are his hands warm? What is the quality of his voice? Notice everything you can notice, but without thinking you know something about what these observations mean, and without judging or labeling. Simply see and hear and smell and touch. We have to be awake and asking inner questions; Who is this child? What are his needs? How can I serve him? When observing a child pay attention to the details.

For example, an observation could be; "This child does not speak the sounds 'R' or 'L.' A judgment might be, "This child has immature speech." "She bumped into furniture or children two times today, and four times yesterday," is an observation. "Clumsy" is a judgment. Practicing observing without judging might be an activity a group of colleagues would work on together.

Another exercise you can take up, when the child is no longer present, is to create a detailed inner picture of the child. At the end of the day try to picture inwardly what you observed. See if you can create a full picture with all the details -from memory - in your mind's eye. Details, images, movement gestures of the child, warmth, shapes, colors, sounds, everything you can recall. Play activities, drawing themes, the way she holds the fork or crayon – all aspects of the child. Include interactions you had with him, and he had with other children. And notice what you cannot recall. If there are gaps, try again the next day. Try filling out the picture. This will train your faculty for observation and recollection. The idea is to learn to allow the child to reveal itself to you.

And then let it go. Un-think these images, in a sense. Make the images go out of your mind's eye. You have built up a series of images, now dissolve them into nothing and leave them to rest in the care of the spiritual beings.

Through these practices we can develop qualities in our selves of sensing in a new way. We begin to meet the child in a new and direct way and start to really see him, and start to see his becoming. Instead of seeing the problems, we start to see the potential in the child. We develop a sense organ that has been asleep and needs exercise to awaken. We are practicing empathy. What does it feel like to be this child with his particular features and characteristics? We cultivate connecting through our interest and attention. Then with enthusiasm and warmth, we welcome the child into our heart. Through compassion and empathy, through this relationship of heart to heart, we open up to the child, and they open to us. This is the healing impulse. And this is a deep connecting without judging of our fellow human being. And sometimes, sometimes we can experience a flash of understanding, a feeling of knowing exactly what is needed, a sense of intuition, and we know that what we know is right.

There is tremendous spiritual help for us in this connecting with the true needs of the child. Consciously including true images of the child in your active meditative life invites the spiritual hierarchies to participate. First, create a mental image of one or another of our clear and true observations of the child before going to sleep in the evening. Accompany the image with a question – What does this child need from me? How can I serve? Then create an expectant silence, an active silence for the spiritual beings to speak into. Wait and listen and see if answers come. Pay attention for an answer, it might not come in a way you think. It might be that several days later a friend suggests you read a particular book that, it turns out, has just what you needed for that child. Or perhaps, the next day one of the other children says something that you realize if exactly what you needed as an idea for helping the child. Be open to everything because the answer might come from anywhere.

The more we understand stages of child development down into the details, the greater is the possibility of receiving intuitions to guide our support for the child's growth. Continually trying to deepen our understanding of the developing consciousness and physiology of the child, along with true and clear observing act like beacons attracting intuitions which will be of service to our work with the child.

When we hold a child in this way, our daily interactions with him are all the more vital and awake. Both teacher and child are enlivened by this, and their souls are enriched by the deep connection and openness they share.

The Pedagogical Law

Rudolf Steiner described a process that he called the pedagogical law. This law explains how the four human bodies interact in educating each other within a given person, and from one person to another. The Spirit I educates the soul, which in turn imprints itself upon the etheric body, and finally the etheric forms the physical. This happens within the human being, and it happens between an adult and child. For the young child, the physical body has been born, and the etheric body is in a sort of embryonic time, therefore the adult must especially look to caring for his soul and etheric bodies which are most active in education the bodies of the young child. Again, in simple terms, the adult's etheric body is educating the young child's physical body during those most formative years, the time from birth until seven years old. And the adult's soul, or astral body, is educating the young child's etheric body which is in a heightened stage of development towards its birth at approximately age seven.

Nurturing the Etheric Body

The etheric body is the source of vitality and health, and it is where habits live. So what can be done to order and nurture one's etheric body? The etheric body is infinite energy and health, so it is more a matter of making sure the etheric forces can smoothly flow into the physical body and the soul. In a certain sense, the etheric forces are the fuel for the will. In the physical realm, the etheric is health and vitality for the body that the will uses as vehicle. In the soul, the etheric forces are energy for willed thinking and awareness, and energy for willed intention and resolve.Some basics for caring for the physical side of your etheric body are rest and nutrition. Enough sleep is essential, and the more of those hours of sleep that are before midnight, the better. What about a short nap after the children leave, or for parents, when the child is napping? Laying down and putting your feet up for five or ten minutes can work wonders for maintaining energy levels and health. Do you eat food that supports your body? There is so much so-called food around the world these days that actually takes away essential nutrients from the body and creates serious health deficiencies. Most prepared and packaged foods, even the organic whole grain kind, are not giving you what your body needs. What about fresh, organic foods, whole grains, and grass-fed animals for any meat and dairy products?

On the soul side of the etheric body, we can practice creating order and organization in our lives. Planning is a discipline that supports etheric forces streaming into the human soul. Finishing activities that we start is an inner discipline that supports the etheric body, and it supports the functioning of the liver, the seat of the etheric body in the human body. Creating a life of balance is important. There are many teachers who wear themselves out with this committee, and that extra meeting, and that other committee, and preparing until well past midnight for the following day, and who every Saturday are in the kindergarten doing those extra wonderful things for the children. They come Sunday to do extra cleaning. The don't have the healthy life of rhythm that they advise the parents to create in their home life. They hardly even have a home life. At faculty meetings, they remind the others how exhausted and burned-out they feel. Hmmm? What a surprise! We cannot allow burnout and exhaustion to live in us, for the sake of the children we need to replace those with inspiration and enthusiasm.

What sort of balance do you have in your own life? Do you give over your entire life to the school? Are you at the resentful stage yet? What nourishes you? What are your passions? Do you make the time to experience practicing these passions? If you don't take care of yourself, who will? No one can.

Rhythm and balance are essential for everyone, teachers and parents included. Often what was a passionate hobby or activity is lost in distant memory. I say; remember your passion, and practice it! If you are a lover of novels, make sure to make the time in your rhythm for the enrichment they provide. Music anyone? Play your instruments, and go see concerts. Just do it. You will discover that every aspect of your life is revitalized.

Did you know that nature is all around us, even in cities, What about a walk outside? A half hour walk per day not only gives keeps active your connection with nature, with the elements, it also gives you relaxed time to let your thoughts wander, and it can cure just about any physical ill. Really.

An additional activity one can take up as a source of renewal for your etheric forces is projective geometry drawing in which one is actually rendering on paper images of the working of etheric forces. Making projective geometric drawings serves to order and strengthen your own etheric forces.

Purifying the Astral Body

Back, back, back, in the back of your mind are you learning an angry language?
Tell me, boy, boy, boy, are you tending to your joy, or are you just letting it vanquish?
Yeah, back, back, back, in the dark of your mind
where the eyes of your demons are gleaming
Are you mad, mad, mad about the life you never had
Even when you are dreaming?...

When you sit right down in the middle of yourself
You're gonna wanna have a comfortable chair.
So renovate your soul before you get too old 'cuz you're gonna be housebound there
When you're old you fold up like an envelope and you mail yourself right inside
Yeah, and there's nowhere to go except out, real slow
Are you ready, boy, for that ride?
(excerpt from the song *Back, Back, Back* by Ani Difranco)

The Six Basic Exercises

When we turn to steps we can take for working on our soul, we look to practices that lead to enhanced awareness and self-direction in our own thinking, feeling and willing. Rudolf Steiner laid out "Six Basic Exercises," or "Six Subsidiary Exercises," that he saw as a precondition for any spiritual development, and that are foundational for the transformation of the soul's three faculties. These exercises are to be done over a period of six months. For an in-depth description, I suggest Steiner's *Guidance in Esoteric Training*, pages 19-24.

The first exercise concerns the development of an ability to focus the thinking on what you choose rather than ride the runaway train of everyday thinking. Practice concentrating your thinking on a particular object for five minutes every day. We learn how to put will in thinking. Next is choosing an activity that is utterly meaningless, and doing it at the same time every day. Thinking must be present in the will to accomplish this. The third exercise is to develop the equanimity whereby the feelings that one experiences are not the motivation for action. We learn to feel our feelings, but not be overcome by them. This equanimity exercise strengthens the heart chakra. It involves bringing thinking and will forces into one's feeling life. This becomes more possible after also working on the thinking and will exercises above. If we develop equanimity, we can operate from a place of responding rather than a reactive basis for actions. This is an essential quality for anyone who ever interacts with people of any age, and what an example we could be for the young children. Positivity is next. We try to develop a sense for seeing what can be learned in even unpleasant situations as we try to put our attention on the positive aspects of experiences. Open-mindedness is the fifth exercise. We meet the ideas from others as if they are true, and let go of all thinking about what is possible or not, and we give those ideas genuine consideration. *What if what I think is the opposite of what is? Can I be in wholehearted, non-judgmental interest?* It is more than holding back judgment, it is truly allowing the new idea to be valid.

I am born a prejudiced person, and freedom for prejudice in my thinking is something I have to achieve during life.
And how can I achieve it? The one and only way is this: instead of taking an interest merely in my own way of thinking and in what I consider right, I must develop a selfless interest in every opinion I encounter, however strongly I may hold it to be mistaken.... The more he develops a social interest in the opinions of other men, even though he considers them erroneous – the more light he receives into his thinking from the opinions of others... (R. Steiner, *The Inner Aspect of the Social Question,* lecture 2, 2/11/1919)

The sixth exercise is finding the harmony that weaves the five previous exercises together with each other, and feeling the calm state of soul that arises. These exercises in themselves are wonderful steps to developing finely tuned soul capacities. Along with them, Steiner offered practices to develop an awareness of the subtle etheric energies working in and around the human body connected to thinking, feeling and willing. These are an essential part of the Six Basic Exercises though they are often overlooked.

After a daily practice of the first exercise, an endeavour is made to become fully conscious of that inner feeling of firmness and security which will soon be noticed by paying subtler attention to one's own soul; the exercise is then brought to a conclusion by focusing the thinking upon the head and the middle of the spine (brain and spinal cord), as if the feeling of security were being poured into this part of the body. (R. Steiner, Guidance in Esoteric Training, p. 20

Following the second exercise, *with subtle attentiveness, we become conscious of the feeling of an inner impulse of activity in* the soul; we pour this feeling into the body, letting it stream down from the head to a point just above the heart. (R. Steiner, *Guidance in Esoteric Training*, p. 20

Along with the third exercise, *Above all, if subtle attentiveness is maintained, an inner tranquillity in the body will one day become noticeable; as in the two cases above, we pour this feeling into the body, letting it stream from the heart, towards the hands, the feet and, finally, the head. This naturally cannot be done after each exercise, for here it is not a matter of one single exercise but of sustained attentiveness to the inner life of the soul. Once every day, at least, this inner tranquillity should be called up before the soul and then the exercise of pouring it out from the heart should proceed.* (R. Steiner, *Guidance in Esoteric Training*, p. 21

And with the fourth exercise, the person *will gradually notice a feeling creeping into him as if his skin were becoming porous on all sides, and as if his soul were opening wide to all kinds of secret and delicate processes in his environment which hitherto entirely escaped his notice. The important point is to combat a very prevalent lack of attentiveness to these subtle things. If it has once been noticed that the feeling described expresses itself in the soul as a kind of bliss, endeavours should be made in thought to guide this feeling to the heart and from there to let it stream into the eyes, and thence out into the space in front of and around oneself. It will be noticed that an intimate relationship to this surrounding space is thereby acquired. A man grows out of and beyond himself, as it were. He learns to regard a part of his environment as something that belongs to him.* (R. Steiner, *Guidance in Esoteric Training*, p. 22*)*

When one practices the fifth exercise, *he will notice creeping into his soul a feeling as if something were becoming alive, astir, in the space referred to in connection with the exercise for the*

*fourth month. This feeling is exceedingly delicate and subtle.
Efforts must be made to be attentive to this delicate vibration in
the environment and to let it stream, as it were, through all the
five senses, especially through the eyes, the ears and through the
skin, in so far as the latter contains the sense of warmth.* (R.
Steiner, *Guidance in Esoteric Training*, p. 23*)*

*In the sixth month, endeavours should be made to repeat all the
five exercises again, systematically and in regular alternation. In
this way a beautiful equilibrium of soul will gradually develop.*
(R. Steiner, *Guidance in Esoteric Training*, p. 23

A consistent practice of both parts of these exercises leads to
sharpened powers of attention, strengthened force of will and
general feelings of calmness and readiness for whatever might
come next. A calm energy begins to permeate the person who
practices these exercises in their totality. For a teacher of young
children, several qualities of soul are especially helpful -
reverence, patience, calmness, and responsiveness - and these are
all supported by a practice of the Six Basic Exercises

Developing the suggested awareness of the movement of energy
within the exercises is a training in sensing the subtle energies at
play in the human being, first within one's self, and then with
practice, outside yourself in others. It is a training for
experiencing the activity of etheric forces, a training to begin to
observe the non-sense perceptible.

Reverence and Gratitude

Children have a natural awe and real reverence for all they
encounter. They are filled with wonder at new sense experiences.
These feelings arise out of a deep connection to all in the child's
environment. Adults don't naturally feel that deep connection -

they have to cultivate those feelings. They diminish in us as we develop and the intellect takes hold. There is a practice that can re-enliven feelings of connection to the world out of gratitude. A basic practice for many people is a daily remembering of the relationship we have as human beings to the four elements. It aids the developing of reverence.

First thing in the morning, as you awaken, think of how you are grateful for water. It is in fact the water of life. As you wash your face and drink a sip, remember that without water there is no life. Then take a deep breath, and feel your connection to the airy element. We breathe from the moment of our birth until death. Without air we would not breathe. Look out the window, step outside, and greet the golden sun. The fire element is our source of light, warmth and transformation. It is essential to a general feeling of well being. And then the ground we walk on. Thanks to the earth herself! The earth gives us the very substance of our body. We live within and depend upon the four elements. In the rushing of modern life, it is so easy to take the elements for granted, but we can practice gratitude for them each and every day.

Imitation and Changing Ourselves

We know that imitation is the natural learning mode for the young child. All the sense impressions, all the experiences, all the "images" the young child receives are soaked up by them in an unconscious way and help to form him. Steiner described imitation as a sort of bodily religion arising from a sense of joy and wonder toward all experiences and sensation. Especially for the young child, the very being of the person is what is most imitated and what has the deepest impact on their development in many areas of development. Our attempting to better ourselves has significant impact on the child. Our striving for self-development is worth imitating. So then the very striving of the adult to develop new capacities penetrates deeply into the developing child and can bear fruit much later in life. *These are qualities I want to develop further in myself and am actively engaging my will on this path.* Indeed it is a path of development for the human being who is striving toward consciousness.

One area where we can attempt to educate ourselves is in our speaking and communicating, as discussed in previous chapters. It is challenging to be aware of one's own true needs and values and be able to communicate those. It is challenging to connect with the real needs of the other. True listening and empathy is challenging to practice, realize, and to experience. Often we slip into judgmental thinking and speaking, or blaming, or solving another's challenges unasked, or reacting rather than responding, or feeling responsible for another's feelings, or, or, or....*The idealizing of thinking, speaking and action provides the human being the possibility of creating new connections.* (R. Steiner, Prague 1922, *The Waking of the Human Soul and the Forming of Destiny,* p. 9)

To be fully aware that the human being is not merely physical, but is a spiritual being in a physical body – out of this awareness arises respect for the other as a spiritual being. Thinking, speaking and action based on this attitude is the idealizing that brings us into greater connection to other human beings, and to the spiritual beings.

For our own adult development it is important to connect with our own feeling life, and for the young children, our example in doing that is important as well. Even though their astral body is still years away from its birth, the examples impressed on the child gestate as potential for the child's future. The work of developing communication skills and tools for resolving conflicts in a healthy way is a life-long learning. It is important for the children to experience our working on ourselves in these areas.

Finding Joy

Pleasure and delight are the forces that most properly enliven and call forth the organs' physical forms.........The joy of children in and with their environment, must therefore be counted among the forces that build and shape the physical organs. They need teachers that look and act with happiness and, most of all, with honest, unaffected love. Such a love that streams, as it were, with warmth through the physical environment of the children may be said to literally "hatch" the forms of the physical organs. (R. Steiner, *The Education of the Child, pps.21/22)*

Children thrive in the presence of devoted caregivers who enjoy life and caring for children. This is the foundation for healthy development and learning. Young children learn primarily through imitation/empathy and, therefore, need to be cared for by people with integrity and warmth who are worthy of being imitated. To put it simply; a teacher of young children should live and teach with joy and love.The young child as wholly sense organ experiences not only the sense-perceptible world, but also the feelings and even thinking of those in his surroundings. Fear and anxiety in the adults are experienced in an immediate way by the young child. Fears in the adults around them yield anxious children. The modern world is cold, hard and hurried, and warmth is required for development of any kind. How can we create an atmosphere of warmth in our kindergartens and early childhood centers and home care situations when today's world is so full of fear? Governments and advertisers play on this to the best of their abilities. The children of today are surrounded by the fears of the adults, and the world of the adults is filled with more and more fears and anxiety. This atmosphere of fear in the environment of the young interferes with their physical development and leads to physical hardening. The path to overcoming this environment of fear is the path toward joy and trust and the benefits are experienced by the adults and the young child. And make no mistake; it is a *path* of development, an effort of engaged will forces, to find joy.

Fears create boundaries and loss of connection between people, and between a person and her body. Allowing fear into one's soul leads to a reactive mode of behavior based on old habits. Fear does not allow for connection with a higher self. When we let fear into our soul, we allow our double to take over, our pattern of behavioral habits. Fear is always about the future. We can only be afraid of something that has not yet occurred. All fear is connected to the unknown, the not-yet.

On the physical level, fear creates a rushing of blood to the heart and a quickening of heart beat. Fear is a contracting, a constricting, even of the blood vessels. From a neurological perspective, it is our reptile brain system that is operant in fear situations. Ongoing chronic fears result in a continual state of "should I fight or should I run?" Fear also results in physical and chemical responses. Blood rushes to the heart from the limbs. The limbs feel cold and heavy. We tend to hold in the breath. In fear and anxiety states, our bodies produce more cortisol which speeds up our reactions. A continuous supply of cortisol in the bloodstream can lead to serious chronic health issues and has been implicated as causal in various cancers. Fear is a stress situation that triggers sympathetic nervous system responses creating a preparedness for fight or flight. The body becomes hyper-aware and digestion is hindered. (see Chapter 3)

Fear and anxiety are cold and prevent connection and growth. Love is by definition a warmth connection, whereby growth is supported. Where there is fear, love cannot find a footing. And the children need to experience the love and warmth of the adult, the kindergarten teacher, the parent, so they feel welcomed and can reveal their gifts and unveil their true nature. Warmth is the nourishment needed for human becoming. Empathy is an antidote for fear. Empathy is love and it is warmth. It arises out of interest in the other, and appreciation and enthusiasm for who they are. *I am connected with you, I feel what you are feeling, yet I don't lose my own center.* It is always a question of finding a balance.

There are so many fears that impinge on the life of adults in our time, and fears that impinge on teachers' work with young children. They include fear of children's injuries, fear of lawsuits, fear of not enough money, fears of illness and death, fear of our own inadequacies. Am I making a difference? Is it worth all my efforts? There are fears of tree climbing, fear of candles, fear of childhood diseases...what are your fears?

The adults' mood of fear results in the child being divorced from life, from reality and from possibilities; they are hindered from meeting their destiny. The atmosphere of fear leads to hardening of the physical body at a young age, and antisocial qualities entering into the life of the young child. In the child, fear interferes with the possibility of play, his primary venue for developing social skills and mastering their own fears. Anxious children have difficulty entering into free creative play with others. When the adults in the environment are anxious and fearful, the young child experiences that tension and lives within it. Children who live in a sea of anxiety don't feel safe and have no clear (inner) boundary between what is play and what is harm. True play can only live when the environment feels safe to the child. Then protective and defensive behaviors are at a minimum. The child can embrace and explore the physical and social world through play. True play can be a means to overcome fears and grasp the world. Play serves as a venue for learning to cope with life. There is a vicious cycle at work here. To play requires an atmosphere of security. One has to feel safe. No safety, no play. No play, no grasping of social dynamic.

In play, we are safe and so we can be vulnerable. If a child is in an environment where they feel safe and nurtured and WITHOUT anxiety, then play is possible and the child is open to embracing the world and other human beings. A tense and anxious atmosphere for a child evokes defensive behaviors and a closed-off gesture that is self-perpetuating. (See the section in Kim John Payne's *Simplicity Parenting* on 'Soul Fever.')

Children need a lack of external control over their play. Yet out of fear, how much controlling of the children's play is inflicted. Stuart Brown (The Institute for Play) says that all social creatures need a rough and tumble element in their play to become truly social in their community. Can we allow this in our young children's play? The children, especially the boys, need to come up against each other in a physical way. Through this they are learning about themselves and the social world. We have to find a comfortable balance for ourselves between physical safety and allowed rough play. This is about our inner attitude; we may have to stretch ourselves and learn to become less anxious.There are many inner exercises one can practice to ameliorate fear and develop joy and trust. It can be a part of a personal daily practice in self development. Fear and love both live in the realm of the heart. The key to working with fear is striving for a balance in the heart, and becoming more conscious from within one's heart, learning to think with the heart. Fear is the opposite of joy - both are heart-centered attitudes. A practice that balances and strengthens one's heart chakra is an antidote for fear. The Equanimity exercise (the third Basic Exercise) helps us say to our self, "Yes there is fear. I feel the fear. And in my observing it, I do not have to be ruled by it. What is this fear trying to tell me?" If we can merely focus attention on the fear itself, rather than on what it is we are fearing, it dissipates. Our attention is the warm light of the sun which melts the ice of fear.

To meet fear, we have to consciously draw our self into the heart, to think with the heart and expand our consciousness. A regular practice of Steiner's "Main Exercise" (in *Guidance in Esoteric Training*), or the "Heart Meditation" as described in Ehrenfried Pfeifer's *Heart Lectures* is one way to alleviate fear. Both of these exercises develop in us a capacity to experience the center and the periphery at the same time, which creates a peaceful and joyful feeling permeating one's whole being.. The center and the periphery are polar opposites and yet are the same location. The human heart encompasses both - and lives in both. This may seem confusing, and it is until one takes up the practice to be able to experience it for oneself. We can develop a capacity to expand our thinking to include center and periphery as the same.

Psychotherapist David Richo offers a tool for processing fear when it could immobilize or destabilize us that he calls the Triple A approach. First **Admit** to yourself that there is fear, and tell at least one other person you trust. Talk about the fear and acknowledge it - let it in, admit it. Then **Allow** yourself to fully feel the fear. Finally, **Act** as if, or so that, the fear cannot stop or drive you in any way. Richo says this '3 A' approach works for any sort of neurotic reactions one has.

Another aspect of the path toward overcoming fear and finding joy is learning to embrace one's karma. One can ask of the situations that come toward one in life's vast unknowableness, "What am I being asked to develop in myself? What new capacities can I develop? What old habits of reaction can I now transform?" This requires a true attitude of openness and meeting all aspects of life as questions. The future is unknown, and if I can embrace it as it moves toward me I will find joy. Joy comes from an attitude of gratitude toward what life brings, even the painful things. I can meet life's challenges and pain as an opportunity for growth, for developing new capacities. It is a given that life will offer us pain and challenges. It is up to each of us how we respond. Seeing the opportunity for inner growth that these challenges offer can be a tremendous boost for our self development.

It can be counted on that we will experience challenges, life is reliable that way. Things change and end, and sometimes they don't go exactly as we planned. Inevitably we will experience some pain as a part of life, and sometimes things just won't seem fair. Can we learn to accept life as including these features, and develop our capacity for meeting those sorts of situation as opportunities for our own growth? This accepting and embracing of the events that come to us develops in us the compassion, strength, loving kindness and depth that mark our becoming more and more truly human. Healthy adults recognize their own feelings, and process them, yet they are not compelled to act from the feeling. Instead of "I am angry," how about, "I feel angry" as an inner gesture to develop? Developing the capacity to let go is an important step. Letting go of blaming and making someone wrong is an obstacle to fully resolving a challenging situation.

When the child in your care finds a safe haven to be himself, when he feels safe and comfortable, then it is possible some behaviors will appear that you don't like. The haven of a 'holding environment' welcomes the child into processing and resolving the challenges that they face and have faced in their earlier years.

When I connect with my joy, then I can guide the young child into a life of connecting and relating. I create an environment of love and joy in which the child can grow healthy physical organs. An environment of joy attracts the incarnating ego of the young child toward a healthy connection with earthly life.

Start Now

Whatever exercises you decide to take up, create a daily rhythm for their practice. There is strength that comes from daily rhythm that aids in the doing of the practice. Steiner said rhythm replaces strength, and in this context, rhythm allows your practice to become part of your daily routine and you stop having to remember to do it, to force yourself to do it. The late Rene Querido, former director of Waldorf Teacher Training at Rudolf

Steiner College, after a lecture on meditation was asked which is the best meditation practice to take up. His answer; "The best meditation is the one you do."

The term 'practice' implies that you have to do it over and over again so that you improve. So take up a practice and do it over and over for days and weeks and months and see what it leads to. With a daily practice, over time things can develop.

'Negative Capability' - that is when man is capable of being in uncertainties, mysteries, doubts, without any irritable reaching after fact and reason. (John Keats)

We are trained by the modern world to be able to have what we want when we want it, but with self-development, we have to learn to wait for the changes in ourself. And we have to learn to wait for inner experiences, wait for intuitions. We can't expect to have an 'instant messaging' chat with spiritual beings. They don't do cell phones and internet, theirs is a different sort of network and time works differently in their domain. The waiting for our inner experiences to mature and bear fruit is already a step toward developing valuable soul qualities including patience and open-mindedness.

We must be able to wait. We must be able to give experiences the opportunity to mature in our soul. (R. Steiner, *An Exercise for Karmic Insight*)

There are two times of day especially conducive to meditative activities. These are the threshold times just after waking from sleep, and just before going to sleep. At these times when our consciousness is at the threshold, the veils between the worlds are thinner. Creating and releasing images just before sleep gives spiritual beings substance for their work. When we sleep, our spirit I is in the spiritual world with other spiritual beings and they work together on various projects. When we awake, if we create a quiet listening space, we may receive progress reports, or we may hear from someone else later in the day or week something pertinent to our questions. Upon waking is a powerful time to practice re-connecting with the elements that make up and sustain our physical world and re-membering gratitude, wonder and reverence.

As you practice your chosen practice and walk upon your path, there may arise fear of what you might find if you honestly look at yourself. To overcome that fear one needs to have the courage for seeking self knowledge, the courage to know yourself. It may be that there are aspects of yourself that you find that you are not happy with, you might not want to keep looking. You may be filled with doubt toward yourself about what you discover. We need to kindle and rekindle our own enthusiasm for change. Change can be scary because at least we are used to the way it is, and change is to the unknown. Take a chance - you don't have to be merely content with what is. you can transform. Allow yourself to change and allow yourself to notice the changes you make in yourself. Habits CAN change, but this requires awake and creative thinking for yourself. This means digesting, contemplating, and openly considering what comes to you, relating it with what you already know and have experienced, and seeing what answers come to you.

Various suggestions have been made in these pages that can be a foundation for self-education and changing one's own habits. Through these practices one can begin to become a *responder* rather than a *reactor*. There are various other exercises one can take up that include meditation with mantric verses as a way to connect with the cosmic wisdom that is streaming towards us all the time. Rudolf Steiner offered many, many such practices and mantras that can become part of your daily practice if you so choose. This is not intended to be a book on meditation; it is focused on the awakening in the will, the transformative potential that makes one a true human being.

When we awaken ourselves through self education we have a solid foundation from which to connect with the other. Underlying all of the work toward true connecting and relating is the spiritual activity of self development. We begin to recognize that there is a part of our being that can learn the lessons our life delivers, the questions our karma brings to us. We live with these karmic questions, embracing the questions and challenges as opportunities to enhance connection and develop trust in ourselves and trust in the activity of the spiritual world which is all around us.

Insofar as we unite ourselves with the spirit of the universe, we become whole human beings, we receive impulses to search as human beings for the other human being, rather than pass one another by without understanding. The more we merely describe physical matter and then apply such descriptions to human beings, the more social life will be torn apart; the more we unite ourselves with the spirit, the more our hearts will open to other human beings. In this way, an education which allows the spiritual in the other human being to be found, provides the foundation for human love, human compassion, and human service, in the true sense of the word.
Rudolf Steiner - April 17, 1924, Bern, Switzerland

Chapter 8

A Beginning

The wheel is turning and you can't slow down
You can't let go and you can't hold on
You can't go back and you can't stand still
If the thunder don't get you then the lightning will

Won't you try just a little bit harder?
Couldn't you try just a little bit more?

Round round robin run around
Gotta get back where you belong
Little bit harder, just a little bit more
Little bit farther than you than you've gone before
(Robert Hunter)

You have come to the end of this book, and my hope is that it can be a beginning for you. I hope it has been and will continue to be helpful for you.

I have tried not to offer recipes and scripts, but instead some basic principles that you can use to become more conscious n your relating to young children, and determine what to do or say in a variety of situations. Central in the work I have described is making what is instinctive into possibilities for awareness and consciousness.

Many present difficulties and much that is chaotic in our era, become quite explicable when one knows that the task of our era is to raise that which is instinctive to the plane of consciousness. What is instinctive in us happens to a certain degree by itself, but to achieve a conscious result one must make an inward effort, above all, to begin to think truly with one's whole being.
(R. Steiner, *Social and Antisocial Forces*, p. 2)

Central aspects of the thinking I have offered in this book include:

1. The development of the capacity for active observing in the adult. Then we can begin to see what is truly needed.

2. The basic mechanism for learning is the will - all education is education of the will, both in the adult herself, and then in the child. How can we foster situations in which the will of the young child can take hold? How can we foster situations where true learning can arise?

3. The primary learning modality for the young child is imitation, so what we do and say, and who we are, as adults standing before them, is of utmost importance.

Finally, I offer four basic principles for all of this to each of us who is our own expert-in-the-becoming.

1. Pay Attention. Become more aware of yourself and your surroundings, as well as the other human being with whom you are interacting.

2. Keep the child's consciousness in mind. Where is he in his own development?

3. Learn to trust in yourself, and your intention to do better.

4. Learn from your experience

The most important thing is to establish an education through which human beings learn once more how to live with one another. Rudolf Steiner, *The Younger Generation,* p. 14

I hope I have inspired you in the way Victor Wooten was inspired when he said; *I should listen to all that you or anyone else has to say. Then I make up my own mind. I choose what I want to believe. And if I'm having trouble figuring out what the truth is, what my truth is, I ask questions, listen, and let experience talk to me.* (Victor Wooten, *The Music Lesson,* p. 192,)

Fambai Zvakanaka

Bibliography

Including both sources for quotes and references, as well as suggested readings:

Rudolf Steiner

Anthroposophy (A Fragment) – Anthroposophic Press, 1996

Anthroposophy, An Introduction - Rudolf Steiner Press, 1983

The Basel Course on Pedagogy, April – May 1920, lecture 13, Also in *Understanding Young Children,* WECAN Press

The Child's Changing Consciousness, Anthroposophic Press, 1988

Education and Modern Life, Garber Communications, 1989

The Education of the Child in the Light of Anthroposophy, Anthroposophic Press, 1996

An Exercise for Karmic Insight, Sophia Audio Books

Guidance in Esoteric Training, Rudolf Steiner Press, 1994

How to Know Higher Worlds, Anthroposophic Press, 1994

Human Values in Education, Anthroposophic Press, 2004

The Inner Aspect of the Social Question, Rudolf Steiner Press, 1974

A Psychology of Body, Soul and Spirit, Anthroposophic Press, 1999

The Realm of Language. The Lost Unison Between Speaking and Thinking, Mercury Press, 1984

Rudolf Steiner in the Waldorf School, Anthroposophic Press, 1996

Social and Antisocial Forces in the Human Being, Mercury Press, 1995

Soul Economy and Waldorf Education, Steiner Books, 1986

The Spirit of the Waldorf School, Anthroposophic Press, 1995

Start Now! A Book of Soul and Spiritual Exercises – Steiner Books, 2004

Study of Man, Rudolf Steiner Press, 1990

Understanding Young Children, WECAN, 1994

The Waking of the Human Soul and the Forming of Destiny, Steiner Book Centre, 1983

The Younger Generation, Anthroposophic Press, 1967

The Zone of the Senses, typed transcript of a lecture from December 30, 1917, Dornach, Switzerland

Child Development

Dinkel, Dana, *WSU professor researches how to speak to children,* (about the work of Raymond Hull) Wichita State Univ. www.wichita.edu/thisis/wsunews/news/?nid=307

Gatto, John Taylor *Weapons of Mass Instruction*, New Society Publishers, 2008

Glöckler, Michaela, *Non-Verbal Education: A Necessity in the Developmental Stages*, translated by Martyn Rawson, in *Waldorf Journal Project #2*

Glöckler, Michaela and Wolfgang Goebel, *A Guide to Child Health*, Floris Books, 1990

Goldberg, Raoul, *Awakening to Child Health I*, Hawthorn Press, 2009

Heckmann, Helle, *Nokken, A Garden for Children*, Nokken, 1997

Klocek, Dennis, *Knowledge, Teaching and the Death of the Mysteries*, Rudolf Steiner College Press, 2000

Konig, Karl, *Man As A Social Being and the Mission of Conscience*, Camphill Press, 1990

Lievehoed, Bernard, *Phases of Childhood; Growing in Body, Soul and Spirit,* Floris Books, 1997

Louv, Richard, *Last Child in the Woods; Saving our Children From Nature-Deficit Disorder*, Algonquin Books, 2008

Meyerkort, Margret and Rudy Lissau, *The Challenge of the Will,* Rudolf Steiner College Press, 2000

Paley, Vivian Gussin , *A Child's Work; the Importance of Fantasy Play*, University of Chicago Press, 2004

Payne, Kim John, *Simplicity Parenting*, Ballantine Books, 2010

Pikler, Emi, *Some Contributions to the Study of the Gross Motor Development of Children, Journal of Genetic Psychology*, 1968

Schaenen, Inda, *The 7 O'Clock Bedtime: Early to bed, early to rise, makes a child healthy, playful, and wise,* Regan Books, 2001

Schoorel, Edmund, *The First Seven Years: The Physiology of Childhood*, Rudolf Steiner College Press, 2004

Sweet, Win and Bill, *Living Joyfully With Children*, Acropolis Books, 1997

van Dam, Joop ,*Understanding Imitation Through a Deeper Look at Human Development*, p. 105, in *The Developing Child: The First Seven Years*; WECAN 2004

Self Development

Cunningham, John, free Compassionate Communication booklet available for download, www.empathy-conexus.com

Klocek, Dennis, *The Seer's Handbook*, Steiner Books, 2005

Selg, Peter, *The Therapeutic Eye; How Rudolf Steiner Observed Children*, Steiner Books, 2008

Richo, David, *Daring to Trust*, Shambala Publications, 2010

Rosenberg, Marshall, *Nonviolent Communication; A Language of Life,* PuddleDancer Press, 2003

Sardello, Robert, *Silence; The Mystery of Wholeness,* Goldenstone Press, 2008

Sardello, Robert, *Freeing the Soul from Fear,* Riverhead Trade, 2001

Thomas, Linda *Chaos in Everyday Life: About Cleaning and Caring,* in *Gateways,* Issue 45, Fall/Winter 2003

Touber,Tijn, *Because God Whispers, Ode Magazine*, July/August 2008

Wells, Rosemary, *Only You*, Viking, 2003

Wooten, Victor L., *The Music Lesson; A Spiritual Search for Growth through Music,* 2006, Berkley Books

What is Restorative Practices? www.iirp.org/whatisrp.php

Websites

Dr. Susan Johnson www.youandyourchildshealth.org

Waldorf Early Childhood Association of North America (WECAN) www.waldorfearlychildhood.org

Dennic Klocek   http://dennisklocek.com

Non Violent Communication www.cnvc.org

Resources for Infant Educarers (RIE) http://www.rie.org